Am I My Mother's Daughter?

A Search for Identity

Julie Stern Joseph

PUBLISHING

JERUSALEM • NEW YORK

AM I MY MOTHER'S DAUGHTER?
A Search for Identity

Published by DEVORA PUBLISHING COMPANY

Text Copyright © 2005 by Julie Stern Joseph

Cover and Book Design: Benjie Herskowitz
Cover Photograph: Rabenko Photography

Cover Photo: The author's mother with the author.

All rights reserved. No part of this book may be reproduced or transmitted in any form or by any means, electronic or mechanical, including photocopying, recording, or by any information storage and retrieval system, without permission in writing from the publisher.

Hard Cover   ISBN: 1-932687-29-7
Soft Cover   ISBN: 1-932687-30-0

Email: sales@devorapublishing.com
Web Site: www.devorapublishing.com

Printed in Israel

Dedications

To my husband Josh: *(Joshua, translated from Hebrew means, a redeemer):*
Incline your ear to me;
Be quick to save me;
Be a rock, a stronghold for me;
A citadel for my deliverance.
For you are my rock and my fortress,
You lead me and guide me as it befits your name
You free me from the net laid for me, for you are my stronghold.
Into your hand, I entrust your spirit;
You redeem me.
Psalm 31: 3-6

To my children, Zachary, Oscar, and Marsha:
Come, my children, listen to me;
I will teach you what it is to fear the Lord.
Who is the one that is eager for life,
Who desire years of good fortune?
Guard your tongue from evil,
Your lips from deceitful speech.
Shun evil and do good,
Seek peace and pursue it.
The eyes of the Lord are on the righteous,
His ears are attentive to their cry.
Psalms 34: 13-16

To my mother-in-law, Norma:
. . . Do not urge me to leave you, to turn back and not follow you. For wherever you go, I will go; wherever you lodge, I will lodge; your people shall be my people and your God my God. Where you die, I will die, and there I will be buried. This and more may the Lord do to me if anything but death parts me from you.
The Book of Ruth, 1: 16-17

To God, the Ultimate Redeemer:
I will sing to the Lord as long as I shall live;
All my life I will chant hymns to my God.
May my prayer be pleasing to Him;
I will rejoice in the Lord.
Psalms, 104: 33-34

Contents

Foreword		7
Acknowledgements		9
Introduction		11
Chapter 1	Marsha	27
Chapter 2	Fall 2003: Clouds	31
Chapter 3	Six Different Doctors in Six Different Offices	38
Chapter 4	Surgery and Post-Op: Waiting Rooms	52
Chapter 5	Who Will Take Care of the Kids?	62
Chapter 6	Funky Mole	71
Chapter 7	Getting Out of Bed	78
Chapter 8	Birthdays	86
Chapter 9	"Go Doctor, Go!"	93
Chapter 10	Family, Friends, Fears and Tears	107
Chapter 11	Countdown to Treatment	111
Chapter 12	Let the Battle Begin!	121
Chapter 13	New Beginnings	132
Epilogue		141
Appendix		147
Resources		150

Foreword

I am saying "Mommy," and she doesn't answer. I say, "Mommy," louder but she is still not answering me. I begin to cry to myself as I ask, "Why won't she speak to me?"

During diagnosis and preparation for surgery, each time I heard my children call or cry for me, that painful memory of yearning for my mother would surface without warning — there was always silence. The rejection I felt was profound and the pain remained, though I understand why my mother did not answer — she was weak and ill. As a child I perceived the problem was me. *Why won't she talk to me?* I hear the echoes and feel the emptiness still.

Now I am the parent with cancer and have young children. On the one hand, I fear imposing pain and silence onto my children. On the other hand, I feel I have been given an opportunity to deal with my sickness with a positive attitude and I hope my children will have a different cancer experience than my own as a child.

I've been told by my mother's sisters that the 'distance' I felt from my mother was never her intention. She only wanted the best for me; she loved me. Perhaps what I sensed as her distance was her pain and anguish concerning her struggle to live. But as a child, this was unknown to me. I grew up feeling loneliness and abandonment, if only there could have been someone to explain to me my mother's love and my mother's illness, but back then, cancer wasn't something you spoke about at the dinner table, it was always referred to in a whisper. In this book, my goal is to express the voice of the child, the child I was, and using that voice is how I will make decisions for myself and my children.

First, my children have Josh—who is a warm, sensitive, responsible, and attentive parent. Second, my mother-in-law will be here to give my children the love and attention that at times may be impossible for me to give. Third, whatever has happened in the recent past and may happen in the next few months, I will survive. I pray that my end is *not* near, that this is simply a new journey, a new experience, and perhaps one day I will know why all this was necessary.

At night I cry and yearn for my mommy's hug of reassurance that everything is going to be okay. I feel lonely and abandoned. I am a novice, unqualified to make decisions.

I struggle to balance the needs of my children with my own. I don't know how to do it all and then I yearn for my mommy. Maybe she would have guided me to become a better mommy, a better wife, a better person. I hear how my children call—I want my mommy!

Many times I panic and have second thoughts. *Why am I subjecting myself to so much toxicity when right now I'm cancer-free? Why must I leave my children to get treatment when I can get a milder chemotherapy treatment in New York and see the children daily?* I ask myself these questions because it's so hard to have confidence in both a treatment and a doctor without evidence that it leads to a cure. I am thirty years old and have to decide on a treatment option with no clear outcome. The only thing clear is that I must do something to prevent the melanoma from returning, even psychologically. I remember what my mother wrote in a note to herself:

> *Why I am going to make it:*
> *1. I don't want to die.*
> *2. My friends, family, and children don't want me to die.*
> *3. All of the prayers will be heard.*
> *4. I'll take any treatment that I have to.*
>
> My Mommy, 1978

So, too, will I. Biochemotherapy is an aggressive treatment. I am going to give it a chance. My mother must have been much braver. She was told from the beginning that she would die. I am told that in the short-term I will live and yet I still weep with fear.

Acknowledgements

There are so many people that I need to thank for helping me during this difficult time. I am grateful to the great team of doctors who continue to help in the present. I thank my block and the Five Towns community for their prayers, support, visits, and meals provided during this time. Josh and I are fortunate to have rabbis and friends who avail themselves on a daily basis.

I would like to thank my editors, Elise Teitelbaum and Danielle Barak, and publisher, Yaakov Peterseil at Devora Publishing for their dedication to my journey. I also want to thank friends and family who helped in the editing process along the way, Barbara Martin, Lori Schlussel, Leora Wechsler, Norma Joseph, Gail Propp, Caroline Schwarcz and my husband, Josh.

I am grateful for the support from both my mother's and father's family. I also thank Josh's family, both in Israel and in the United States. We are also fortunate to have loving and warm siblings: Caroline and David Schwarcz, Pamela and Douglas Stern, Deborah and Marc Zimbler, Leora and Michael Wechsler, Yael and Ami Joseph, and Shanna and Naphtali Joseph.

I am forever indebted to the love given to me by Dr. Norma and Rabbi Howard Joseph. They are the in-laws, the parents that I have always prayed for and the best grandparents in the world.

Thanks to our good friends Linda and Ben whose support for this book made it possible.

Uncle Leonard, where would I be without you? Your constant support enabled me to pick the right treatment and enable me to recover from this disease as best as I can.

I want to thank the three passions of my life, Zachary, Ozzie and

Marsha whose presence continually guides me toward the meaning of life.

Lastly, Josh, my husband, best friend, and love of my life, without you I wouldn't know what the joy of life is about. You are my life and nothing in this world is more important than you. You are my soul mate. I am grateful for your unconditional support of me and especially your written contributions to this book. It means so much to me that you want to be a part of it, even after the cancer is over.

Introduction

I have come to the conclusion that this mess is me.

When I was eleven, I once confronted my father with a question as to why he was not a better parent. Thank God, this question did not ignite his anger and he simply responded:

"Why, what would you like me to be?"

"Well, my friends' fathers play with their kids and do activities with them on Sundays," I said.

"That's ridiculous. That is not a man's job," he replied. "A man's job is to work and to provide food and clothing for his family. I do my job. What you're missing is a mother and it's not my fault that she's dead."

"I'm going to marry a man who will not only provide for my children, but will want to play with them as well!"

"So you're going to marry a homosexual!" he said.

"I will not. I'm just going to find a man who enjoys spending time with his children."

I don't remember how the conversation ended, but I maintained my conviction that I would marry a man who would love his children and whose involvement with them did not end with conception.

My father had a temper and you never knew which question would trigger it. It could have been, "Can I have some money for school?" or, "Are we going to synagogue today?" My father was a yeller and when he shouted it felt like you needed to take cover; the house literally shook. So, initially, I promised I would never raise my voice to my children. I did not want to become someone who yelled. What I later understood about the yelling was that I dispised the content of his words, not the volume. He would verbally humiliate me and rip me into shreds. I swore to do whatever I could to become independent of him.

As I became a more experienced parent, I realized there were times when I needed to change my tone of voice to convey urgency. On those occasions, I feared that perhaps I was becoming my father. It took time for me to realize that my raised tone did not come from exasperation or loss of control; my tones were premeditated and well-planned to sound serious enough that my children would take me seriously.

Before my mother died, she hired a governess to take care of us children. I remember, the night we met, being shown the exact position under my ear where she would pull my hair if I didn't listen. I heard her say it, but I did not expect it to become a daily reality for the next two years of my life.

Every morning we children were expected to drink fresh orange juice with our breakfasts. The pulp would make me gag. Nevertheless, the woman would yank my hair with one hand while simultaneously smacking me across the face with the other until I would submit and drink the juice. It didn't bother her that I would then run to the bathroom and vomit; just having me drink the juice, it seemed, was her personal fulfillment each morning.

It got to be so bad that just the anticipation of the juice each morning would make me gag. Neither I nor my siblings ever told my father about these events. We feared he might agree with the woman's behavior. Maybe my father would agree that I should drink my orange juice and eat string beans and liver. In my six-year old head I rationalized that telling him would only further enrage her and she would come back to beat me for humiliating her in front of my father. I'm sure this was all unknown to my mother.

Introduction 13

Two years later, my sisters and I returned home from summer camp and my father explained that he had to let the woman go. "She was crazy!" he said. "She was charging drugs on our family's pharmaceutical account! I fired her immediately!" My sisters and I looked at each other and began to tell our father all the things she had done to us. My father responded simply and unemotionally, "How was I supposed to know if you didn't tell me. It's not my fault." Why couldn't he just say, "I'm sorry. I'm sorry that I've been preoccupied and depressed over the loss of your mother." I have never forgiven him for his lack of accountability.

I feel the need to place my feelings of anger towards my father in a more appropriate context. To my father's credit he accomplished many wonderful things in his life. He named a high school after my mother as well as a college in the Israeli Negev. He established a scholarship in my mother's name at a yeshiva in Israel, it was also a place that his father had supported greatly in his lifetime. My father helped hundreds of people financially.

My father was passionate in his love for Israel. He purchased a home there with my mother. Near his plot of land were less than ten others — there were no phone lines, but my father felt rich when at his doorstep lay the ocean and the history of Caesarea, named for the Roman Emperor Caesar Augustus by the corrupt Judean king, Herod. It had been a beautiful, fortified city with an aqueduct, fortress, and coliseum.

In this aspect of my father's life, he was a true visionary — Caesarea has grown exponentially. When I was younger, on holidays there was a minyan (congregation of at least ten men) in the post office. It was part of my father's dream to build a synagogue in Caesarea; the last one had been destroyed over 2,000 years ago. Few yearly residents wanted a synagogue but my father was involved in its meticulous planning. He did not live to see the synagogue's inauguration and celebration of its first sefer Torah, during which President Ezer Weizman carried in the sefer torah and spoke. The irony of ironies is that, even though their homes were two blocks apart, he and my father had never gotten along well, perhaps because of the clash between my father's religious and Ezer's secular values.

Another example of my father's Zionist vision was his friendship with Arik Sharon. I remember when he was elected prime minister of Israel in 2000 and I cried. Some people had thought my father "crazy" for his political views, but he was right about Arik, had faith in his character and knew he would one day be prime minister. I think he admired the warrior in Arik. They met when Sharon was fundraising for development of the West Bank. Perhaps I overheard incorrectly, but I remember going into school the next day and telling my teacher that Arik Sharon just asked my father to buy the whole West Bank. I do know that whenever Sharon needed help with a project, my father rushed his side and vice versa.

My father had a good friend whose son had started a Jewish settlement near Nazareth and had appealed to the Israeli government on many occasions for electricity. This young man came to speak to my father about the settlement's condition. My father found money to build a park for the children, and then called Sharon for help. Within a week this settlement had electricity.

I recently came upon the eulogy that Ariel Sharon gave at my father's burial in Caesarea. The following is an excerpt:

> *Stanley always provided assistance and support – openly and possibly even more through anonymous chesed – especially in the field of education, and Jewish education in particular.*
>
> *Stanley was an ardent supporter of Israel – always concerned for its fate, following every development over here in the fields of aliyah, industry, settlement, and security. He was always concerned for Israel's political standing, worried over every little sign of weakness.*
>
> *His greatest pride was the fact that Israel was becoming more and more his permanent place of residence. Even when living abroad, his attachment to this country was complete....*
>
> *This was the man – A very special man. At times we found him difficult to understand, as we are used to sharply-defined lines – either black or white. This man was different: round-edged, cultured, mild-mannered and charming....*

Many people have commented to me on the positive impact my father made on their lives. In the United States, my father contributed to the founding of Albert Einstein College of Medicine, built a wing within Mount Sinai Hospital of Medicine and named a school after my mother, The Marsha Stern Talmudic Academy for Boys.

I know there were good and caring sides to my father, but it's hard for me to forget his verbal maelstroms. A teacher of mine recently said that when one can realize that the "sins" are only symptoms of the "illness," then one can begin to forgive. My problem is that I only knew my father was mentally ill about two years before his death. Until then this moody individual, as I described him, hurt me in several ways. I still cannot tell how much of what he said was a manifestation of his illness.

One thing I would like to clarify is that it was not only the years I spent growing up with him that had been difficult. In addition, the diagnosis itself cracked whatever stability I had. I had been used to this "crazy" person whom I loved nonetheless. But when I found out that some of his behaviors were not reflective of the "true" him then my world fell apart.

In the earlier years after my mother's death, my father had been the center of my world. He was "my daddy," as I used to say lovingly. I regarded him as the ultimate moral and righteous individual. However, as his illness could no longer be concealed (at that point I was still unaware of it) my feelings of love and the benfit of doubt I gave him began to deconstruct. John Steinbeck in *East of Eden* poetically expresses the disappointment in finding out that a father is not the man he was thought to be:

> *"When a child first catches adults out – when it first walks into his grave little head that adults do not have divine intelligence, that their judgments are not always wise, their thinking true, [and] their sentences just – his world falls into panic desolation. The gods are fallen and all safety gone. And there is one sure thing about the fall of gods: they do not fall a little; they crash and shatter and sink deeply into green muck. It is the tedious job to build them up again; they never quite shine. And the child's world is never quite whole again. It is an aching kind of growing."*

The diagnosis was just another trauma in my life, even more so because my family members had chosen to conceal the truth from me. They thought they were protecting me. When the truth came out I had no skills to deal with it, and that was when my first serious depression set in. *If my father was not who I thought he was, who was I?* It was a difficult process to work through and at times I was so depressed that suicide seemed the only option to end the constant pain I was feeling. Luckily with the help of a good psychiatrist and medication I slowly was able to begin to rebuild my world. Though many of the wounds have healed, the scars are still visible.

There are many more secrets, but my purpose is not to expose or hurt, but rather to explain how I survived the impasses and learned to seek out happiness.

What I have learned as a parent from this experience is that family secrets lead to distrust. For that reason alone, Josh and I are open with our children about my illness and treatments. The truth is hard to hear, but I would rather know now than later discover that the images of people I love are a sham.

My mother

My mother developed breast cancer a few months after I was born and was only given a few months to live. I was fortunate that she lived some weeks past my sixth birthday, or I would have no memory of her at all. I remember when she went to the hospital for what would be the last time. I was unaware at the time that my childhood was filled with her coming and going into and out of hospitals. On what proved to be the last occasion, I remember asking my mother two questions: "When is your hair going to grow back?" and, "When are you going to come home?"

In answer to my question, she said, "My hair will have grown back when I return home for your birthday." My birthday passed on March 7, 1979, but my mommy never came home. She died March 28, 1979.

Though her bedroom was filled with bewigged headstands, I loved touching the stubble on her scalp that became so soft. I probably asked much too frequently if I could touch it, and she was not always in the mood to remove the cap that she wore in the house to cover her hair loss. But every so often she would indulge my requests and I would giggle at the gratification.

I had always thought of wigs as something only for cancer patients. I now live in a community where married women wear wigs to cover their hair for religious reasons, modesty among them. I eventually got used to it and realized how ingenious it was of religious women to use this law to make themselves more attractive.

When I first bought my *sheitel* (Yiddish for wig), my son asked me, "Why do you have that hair?" My first reaction to his question was, *maybe he thinks I have cancer,* but then I realized he was only three years old. I simply answered that some religious women cover their hair with wigs. He stood there and thought about it for a moment and then, obviously satisfied, continued whatever he was doing.

My stepmother

When I was eighteen, my father and stepmother announced that our apartment in New York was for sale and we were all moving to Israel. My father had purchased a home with my mother in Caesarea when they were newly married and he actually met his second wife there. The home in Caesarea was going to be the new Stern residence.

All this news came as a surprise to me. I was in my last year of high school and thinking about my own future. It was during the last six weeks of school that I finally had an inkling as to what was going on. My school had a program for seniors called "work-study" where we interned in a profession during the last six weeks of school. A friend of mine got a job at Sotheby's and I remember being at her home and flipping through their recent auction catalog. As I leafed through the pages, I became dumbfounded when I recognized paintings and furniture from my home. At first I thought others had similar furniture but then I realized the paintings were supposed to be originals—Picassos and Chagalls—that for years had been there on the walls of my home.

When I later asked my stepmother about it she tried to avoid the discussion. Instead, she revealed that we were having some financial problems and that was why pieces of art, furniture and so on were for sale. I know I was fortunate that I had spent all of my eighteen years in one home, but now it was clear that the public announcement of my family making *aliyah* to Israel was a camouflage for major financial problems.

The next year and a half I spent in an all-women's Torah study program in Jerusalem. Over that time I would visit my father and stepmother in Caesarea. At that point, my father's relationship with my stepmother was deteriorating. In fact, if I look back far enough, it was evident that their relationship never had a chance. My father spoke a broken Hebrew and his new wife could not speak a word of English. It started to turn sour when he wanted us to call her "mommy." That never took off. I was eleven at the time and annoyed and frustrated that now she was responsible for me. That's how my father would do it. When there was a new governess, babysitter, and now wife, he would say, "The children are your responsibility. Kids, if you have any problems, don't come to me." *Great!* When I would try to have a conversation with her and she wasn't able to understand, I got frustrated and began to speak louder. She would then misinterpret my tone as being disrespectful and reprimand me, which led to my becoming more frustrated.

Their relationship hadn't started off well either. Within the first few months of their marriage she redecorated the whole apartment because she wanted it to be her home and not the home of my dead mother. Then one night at dinner, I made a joke about how ugly a set of bedroom curtains were. Immediately, it went back and forth between my father and stepmother as to who was responsible for the ugly curtains. She got out of her chair, announced that she was leaving and left the room. I wondered, *did that mean she was leaving? Would she really leave?*

My father left the table after her and a few moments later I was eavesdropping on a conversation between them and I heard my father say to her, "Please don't leave me." It was strange for me to hear my father in a vulnerable position. In my eyes, he was god, perfect, but with a lethal temper. I assumed that everyone had to do what he said. Nonetheless, she started leaving their bedroom with a suitcase and pressed the elevator. I don't know what came over me, but I soon followed after and watched as she was taking off her wedding rings while she was waiting for the elevator.

I said to her, "You come into this house and you expect us to immediately love and respect you, when in a second you take your things and leave."

I'm not sure why I said that. Was it because I wanted her to stay or was I fearful of what my father would become without her? Whatever the motivation, what I said made sense to her — even though at other times she claimed not to understand me — and she put down her suitcase and came back into the apartment. She went back to their bedroom where my father lay in despair. My sister Deborah and I followed her and very quickly became their marital counselors. These types of fights would continue for years. Divorce threats became so common that they became hard to take seriously and still Deborah and I had to help them communicate. By the time I was eighteen, I had enough of their dysfunctional relationship and no longer got involved in their fighting. If their marriage was going to fall apart it would be without me.

I returned to New York a year and a half later and began Barnard College in January. My father also returned to the United States, but without my stepmother. For the remainder of his life, a year and a half, my father never knew where she was and he was living in and out of hotels. She only returned to him a month before he died. The funny thing was neither I nor my siblings knew or had any intimation that our father was dying. There had been many times over the past few years when he had spent time in and out of hospitals because of a heart condition. It will always be a mystery as to how she knew the hospital visit on May 9, 1994, would be his last.

I maintained a relationship with my stepmother for some time because she was all I had. My father had done a good job in alienating his family from us, such that I felt I had nowhere else to turn. She told everyone that she loved me as a daughter and that she had brought me up. At the time it made sense. We had spent ten years in the same household, and her promises to care for me unconditionally fulfilled my longing for a mother figure.

When I was twenty-six and gave birth to my first son I finally had a sense of what motherhood was about. It was the first time I really understood unconditional love and self-sacrifice. Then it hit me. That role had not been given to my stepmother. She was never involved in my school or social life. The year and a half before my father's death, I never knew where she was as she was busy running away from him.

Once my father died, she played the poor widow and had pictures placed all over the home of my father and family to display our life of "joy and glamour." She told her audience how she had adopted four children and raised them as her own. She played the song of self-sacrifice, but had never experienced it. Every time we got together I would listen to her lament at how terrible her life was since my father's passing. At one point my father's estate was worth millions. At the time of his death his estate was in debt. My stepmother received the home in Israel, and I and my siblings split a small life insurance policy. My mother had made my father promise before she died that he would establish trust funds for all the children, but during his financial demise he violated those accounts and there was no one to be held accountable. My stepmother said how unfair it was for her and how difficult it was without any money. I would sit there listening on many occasions, sometimes feeling sympathetic to her cries, until I realized that I had more pressing financial concerns.

It was the birth of my first child that taught me what it meant to be a mother and it was painful to realize what I had missed for so many years, but my stepmother did give me one gift free of guilt for which I am forever indebted. When all of our artwork and furniture were being auctioned she forced my father to set aside money in a joint account between me and my stepmother, to pay for college. The fact that I never had to track my father down for money gave me a measure of freedom. I had been depressed in college, but to have that state of mind coupled with concern about how I would pay tuition when my father was hard to find, could have pushed me over the edge.

When my eldest son was a year and a half it occurred to me that the responsibility was always on my shoulders to call my stepmother and find out which country she was in. I felt tired, hurt, and disappointed by the nature of our relationship, so one day I decided I would no longer make a conscientious effort to track her down and call her. I deliberately did not send word that I was doing this but, as of this day, I have not spoken to her in more than three years, which has confirmed my thinking that the relationship was viewed as my responsibility alone.

My sister Deborah and my brother Douglas stayed in contact with my stepmother and she sent a message through them when our second son was born. She gave my sister money to buy my baby a present, but I told my sister she could keep it for herself.

When I was pregnant with my third child and it became public that I also had a malignant melanoma, all of a sudden she tried to contact me through Josh. She offered us money or whatever she could do to show her support. I told Josh to give her my message: *I appreciate your concern, but this is not the time to work out our relationship issues.* I assumed she was too embarrassed to say to people who asked about me, "I don't know. We don't talk anymore." Just as she had kept up a façade in Caesarea that life with my father was grand, to her friends she was playing the role of my mother.

When the melanoma episode was over and I gave birth to my baby girl, she didn't try to contact me. Only in November of 2003, when word got out about the recurrence and partial amputation, did she try to connect once again. This time it was through my brother that I heard she wanted to help me and in the same conversation she had with my brother she asked him, "How many children does Julie have now?" When I heard what she had asked, I said to myself, "Forget it! Talking to this woman has given me more grief than joy and I don't want to give her the satisfaction that I need her help in order to ease her guilt." I made a vow a long time ago: Don't let people into my life who can hurt me, even family members. Regardless of whether a relationship has some merit, if there is pain I no longer want it in my life. I'm tired of being surrounded by dysfunctional people, I want a healthy life for me and my family.

Now my three children have one set of functional and loving grandparents, my husband's parents. My five-year old has yet to figure out that I once had parents too, but when he asks I will explain. Josh and I don't believe in offering extra information. For example, Zachary lived through September 11th and still has no idea about it. To initiate a discussion of my parents would be painful for me. Why let Zach down by telling him people typically have two sets of grandparents — one for each parent — when he thinks that the one set he already has is the best in the world?

Josh

I met Josh when I was twenty-one, just three months after my father died from a heart-related disorder.

Josh and I met the summer after my sophomore year of college. I was traveling in Israel and he was studying at a yeshiva. We courted via the Internet. Josh wrote once a week. I wrote daily. Josh returned home for six weeks during his Passover vacation in 1995. We spent so much time together I was beginning to fall in love with him.

But one event sticks in my mind as the catalyst for my surrender to him. It was April, after the birth of his sister's first son, Avi. I saw the way he looked at Avi and how Josh's eyes glowed. Inside I jumped for joy! *I was right daddy. I finally found a man who loves children and who is not a homosexual.*

Zach

Josh and I were engaged the following October and we married on March 10, 1996, three days after my twenty-third birthday. I was so happy to begin my life with him. Two and a half years later, on December 17, 1998, we were thrilled to have our first son, Zachary. I was in turmoil as to whether I had to name our child for my father because it was the customary and respectful thing to do and yet the thought pained me: *How could I name a child after my father, for whom I held few positive memories?*

Josh found a great compromise. We named him *Zechariah Yisrael*. *Zechariah* means "God remembers" and was a memorial to my father. The combination of *Zechariah Yisrael*, "God remembers His people, Israel," was the emotional expression of my gratitude that God had answered my prayers. Even though my early life had been filled with challenges, I felt grateful to be blessed with a happy marriage and to have an opportunity to begin my own family.

Becoming a mother finally gave me the chance to make a *tikkun*, a correction of the negatives in my childhood. Zachary's father has loved and cuddled him since his birth and I am learning to become the mother I never had.

By the time Josh and I had our first child, I was struggling for role models. I read parenting books voraciously and made Josh watch videos on the subject. Even though our child was only six months old, I would discuss hypothetical parenting situations and almost drive Josh crazy with anxiety over my parenting skills. He came from a *normal* family, with two loving parents, and could not understand what all my hysteria was about. At the time I was in graduate school and working part-time as a teacher in a synagogue. Josh was working many hours both in rabbinical school and as an assistant rabbi of the same synagogue.

When Josh arrived home he would, understandably, want to relax, watch television, and zone out for a while. Sunday was for sports. Josh felt that Zachary did not need to go to the park and should be able to occupy himself by playing alone. However, we had a cute little boy who did *not* play by himself. He wanted attention. At first I rationalized that the problem was me—I was still learning how to be a parent, and without any role models.

Josh, who loved to play with Zachary, could not understand why when he came home from work I wanted him to stop what he was doing and give his attention to Zachary. Josh became frustrated—not with Zach, but with me. He said I was bombarding him with Zach without a minute to rest after a long and hard day. Josh would say, "What do you want from me?" He was doing far more than my father ever did. My father didn't even know how to boil water. Still, I expected more from Josh and didn't know how to explain it to him.

Ozzie

Our second son, Oscar (Ozzie), was born on January 25, 2001. Ozzie's Hebrew name is *Azariah Ze'ev*, which can be translated as "Help of God" or "Strength of God." *Ze'ev* means 'wolf.' Giving Ozzie this name was my prayer of thanks to God for giving me not only the internal strength to persevere like a wolf but the physical strength as well.

I wanted to be the mother I never had, a *good* mother. Our children turned us into better parents. Sundays were no longer devoted to sports on television. Just watching Josh interacting with our children made me fall in love with him again. For the sake of our children, we had to become more active parents. People would look at Josh and me with our boys and comment, "Wow, you guys have so much patience and energy." I would answer, "It has nothing to do with my patience level. This is something my sons need." Josh and I were astonished how few parents engage with their children in play and how so many take for granted that they have a child who is happy to spend play time alone.

Even though there were times when I was still hard on myself — questioning if I was doing enough for my children — I became the mom I had wanted for myself. But in order to fulfill my dream, it was necessary to live long enough so my children could grow up knowing their mother.

My burgeoning self-confidence was shattered in July of 2002 when, while pregnant with our third child, I discovered a weird mole on my foot. I had been vigilant about body-checks since high school even though I didn't believe I would ever have malignant melanoma. If anything, I had been waiting all these years for breast cancer, the disease that took my mother. I received the devastating news in the thirty-fourth week of my pregnancy. The mole was a malignant melanoma and what made me even more distressed was that it was one of the few cancers that could actually pass through the placenta to the baby.

When I was eighteen and put myself in therapy, I had a naive sense that I was going to clean up the mess of my bewildering life. Fourteen years later I'm still in therapy, still dealing with issues from childhood and some new ones along the way. I have come to the conclusion that this mess is me. It's a painful realization. Perhaps others have known this truth for some time, but now I see it.

This "mess" includes the happiness and the abysmal pain; the wife, mother, child, sister; the weakness I feel when I cry and am not understood; and the strength to continue no matter what anyone thinks.

Three weeks before my father died, I placed myself under

psychiatric supervision. My suicidal thoughts were scaring me. I would get myself into crying fits, which once I would start would take hours to stop. The medication I was taking at the time had already begun to help curtail those crying cycles, but my negative thoughts were still there and I carried around my psychiatrist's beeper number in case of further self-abusive thoughts.

I told Deborah how, in synagogue during the Passover memorial for the dead, I was crying and yelling at mommy in my prayers. I said, "Why did you leave me here to deal with all this pain? You're lucky. You got the easy way out!"

Deborah searched for the words my mother had written: Why I am going to live. 1) I don't want to die; 2) My friends, family, and children don't want me to die; 3) All of the prayers will be heard; 4) I'll take any treatment that I have to — that expressed how badly she had wanted to live. Deborah said, "Mommy didn't want to die. She wanted to live. She would have done anything to live."

Immediately I felt my heart pounding and my lungs gasping for air. Guilt overwhelmed me. I was having a panic attack. Mommy not-wanting-to-die had ruined my whole outlook on the world. Now I had to reconsider and was ashamed at how selfish I had been. I felt sick to my stomach. I took a valium to calm down. I felt sad and depressed and had no answers to work out my feelings of chaos and loss of control.

At the cemetery, I cried to my mommy. I told her how sorry I was for taking my life for granted, yet I still couldn't honestly feel there was any reason to live. So I made a deal with her. I told her that if I could not find a reason to live right now, at least I would live for her.

Eight years passed and I had not returned to my mother's grave until the burial of my grandmother, four days before my planned cesarean section with Marsha. I knew I had melanoma, but did not know if it had spread to the placenta or throughout my body. I asked a rabbi, an old friend of our family, if I could go to the burial — because it was uncustomary for pregnant women to go to cemeteries. He answered, no. But then I began to cry, "I need to see my mommy!" — which poses another problem in Jewish custom. You're not supposed to visit another gravesite during one person's burial. My mother's grave was unavoidable, only two graves away, from my grandmother.

He said, *"If you are going to feel comfortable and that your anxiety won't cause distress to the baby then you can go."* I chose to go with fortitude. I had a mission.

After my grandmother's burial, as people were dispersing, I walked over to my mother's grave and once again spoke to her. I apologized that it had been so long since my last visit. Then I showed her Josh, told her about my beautiful boys, and told her of my cancer and the baby I was carrying, how I hoped it would be a girl and considered naming it after her. Finally I reminded her of our conversation eight years earlier when I had said that I would live for her if I could not find anything else to live for.

Then I told her, *"I don't need to anymore. I can finally live for myself. I have found joy. I love my life, my husband, and my children. I understand now how much you wanted to live. Please help me; save me, I need to live. I'm not ready to die."*

CHAPTER 1
Marsha

Many years ago I came across a picture of my mom hugging me in her lap when I was five (see cover). I began to cry. I didn't remember her ever hugging me — I had always doubted how much she loved me despite the stories I was told. I liked hearing the stories about my mother but was also angry because I wanted to have my own memories. It is hard for me to trust and rely on the accounts of others even though they mean well. I wish I could remember more. I wish I could remember her telling me she loved me forever and ever.

Since the melanoma was discovered, everything happened very quickly. My baby was delivered as early as possible, at thirty-six weeks. Nine days later I underwent surgery to have more tissue of my foot removed, a skin graft was taken from my thigh, and a sentinel node biopsy was done to see if the melanoma had spread to my lymph nodes. Unfortunately, when the mole was removed, it was already stage II. Thank God, my lymph nodes were clear and I did not need any post-operative treatment. I was going to live! All I had to do for the next two years was to be carefully monitored by both my dermatologist and my surgical oncologist.

From the moment I heard the good news that the lymph nodes

were clear, my cancer was forgotten and I focused on my new baby girl whom I named for my mother, Marsha. Before the melanoma incident I was not sure whether we would name the baby after my mother. I did not care for the name but the striking coincidence that I had developed cancer on the birth of a baby girl as my mother had developed cancer after the birth of me, really shook me up. I was scared. Was my mother's fate to become mine? I had worked so hard with my children that I wasn't ready to die. I knew I could not protect my children from all life's difficulties, but at least I wanted to protect them from my pain. I did not want my children to grow up without a mother. I knew how difficult it had been for me.

Marsha's birth was a miracle on many levels. The mole with the melanoma appeared and was removed in my third trimester. If this had occurred during my second trimester, I would have been confronted with a moral-religious dilemma. I would have had to choose whether to keep my baby. Doctors recommend abortions to pregnant women with melanoma detected early in their pregnancy because they believe the hormonal activity during pregnancy can accelerate the spread of disease and risk the health of both mother and child.

I am grateful that the mole was found to be a stage-II growth, rather than one that would have compromised my life. Also, the development of the baby was far enough along in the term to have a healthy delivery. We gave Marsha the Hebrew name *Miriam Chaya Devorah*. *Miriam* was my mother's Hebrew name. She died prematurely at thirty-six years. *Devorah* was my grandmother who died at the ripe old age of ninety-six, just a few days before Marsha was born. *Chayah* means life. In naming her, I beseeched the Lord: *May this little one – Marsha – live to the old age of Devorah; may the spirit of my mother come alive in our Marsha; and finally, thank God I am alive.*

When that little girl emerged, she instantaneously became Marsha. She connected me to my mom, not just because we had both experienced cancer, but because I now had a little girl I could *Mommy* the way I wished to have been *Mommied*. After my surgery I was cancer-free, thank God, and Marsha has given me comfort for the loss of my mother. It is almost as if I had waited all these years for my mommy, my Marsha, to come back to me. By having my Marsha, I had hoped that she would become the mirror that I for so long was missing a reflection to tell me that I was a good mother, wife, and person.

I felt blessed. We had our two boys, Zach and Ozzie, and our little daughter, Marsha. The melanoma incident was over. It had happened so quickly but it was already in the past. I had been given another chance at life and could not wait to begin.

July 2003

I'm so excited! Marsha's first birthday is coming up. I'm planning a little party for her at my Aunt Gail's summer home in Atlantic Beach, a few minutes from our house in Lawrence.

As a teacher I have the summer off. Seeing ocean instead of skyscrapers can be refreshing. I can be five minutes from home and yet feel like I'm "away" on vacation, the sound of waves in my ears and the feel of sand beneath my feet.

Why am I so excited about Marsha's birthday? I never made a big deal about either of my boys' first birthdays. The idea of a party for a one-year-old is silly. The other one-year-olds don't even notice — it's for the adults. But something is different about Marsha's birthday.

Since my mother's family was in Atlantic Beach for the summer, many showed up for Marsha's cake. My sister and her husband brought their kids and my brother and his wife came for the day from the city. I had invited my sister in the past to Zach's parties and there had always been a reason why she couldn't make it. But on the day of Marsha's birthday, everyone showed up — including many of my cousins.

Josh took ten pictures of Marsha and me, though I'm usually the family photographer and he is the videographer. I often make Josh take pictures of me kissing and hugging my children so if one day they should forget or, if God forbid something ever happened to me, they will have these pictures as proof of my love. I only wish pictures could express more. If my pictures had a caption they would say: *You children are my life, my spirit, the greatest gift God has ever given me.*

I then pray in my own words: *God, please let me live long enough to help my children grow. God, please don't take me away from them. I've just begun to experience joy. I love it. It's the best feeling in the world. The joy fills up my years of hollow loneliness. Life is good. Thank you, God.*

Around the time I went to see my surgical oncologist who examined my foot and lymph nodes for irregularities. He asked me, "What was the date of your surgery?" I paused and then told him I couldn't remember. "I guess I completely blocked it out. I remember Marsha being born on July 19, 2002, but anything after that is a blur." He told me it was understandable not to remember and checked his chart. The surgery had been performed July 28, 2002. A chill went down my spine as memories of that day flooded my brain. I finally realized my cancer experience had been suppressed and sublimated with Marsha's birth.

Something felt surreal. Outwardly we were all celebrating Marsha's birthday, but inwardly everyone was celebrating my recovery. Here I was, alive, a year later, and I had something special to show for it: Marsha. My mom's sisters were celebrating the first birthday of their sister's granddaughter and namesake. Everyone was happy. I wondered who else noticed the clouds of cancer swirling in the distant background.

CHAPTER 2 – Fall 2003
Clouds

September

Josh, an Orthodox rabbi, became the new director of a non-profit Jewish organization and I began full-time teaching—excited but also fearful, having worked close to home for three years. I would now have to commute outside the neighborhood, an hour there and back.

Ozzie, who was two, would go to school on the bus. My babysitter would have to show up by 7 o'clock in the morning for me get to work on time. She would be responsible to get both boys dressed and put them on the bus. I asked her to sleep over Monday through Thursday to avoid having a panic attack before her arrival. I felt guilty about leaving the boys and so each night I made their lunches, packed their book bags, wrote notes to their teachers, and picked out their clothing for the next day.

My new job was from Monday to Thursday; 9 o'clock in the morning to 3 o'clock in the afternoon, five classes each day and home in time to spend a few hours with my children before bed at 7 o'clock. I needed the income, but did not want to sacrifice my children.

Josh was working in the neighborhood—which meant if there was an emergency he could be available. He made it clear that "available" did not mean doing carpool. I asked a friend to pick up Zach from his after school Hebrew program.

Josh and I also set up a busy schedule for our kids. Zach would take Karate twice a week, ice-skating once a week and, together with Ozzie, swimming lessons once a week.

Josh and I felt good. With our new jobs, maybe we had a chance to finally pay all our bills: we had severe debt due to uncovered medical payments. We felt good that things had calmed down but sometimes, when things got settled, all the matters we'd suppressed during hard times began to resurface.

Something was weird. I started to get insomnia and anxiety attacks at night. I rationalized it was the transition to a new pace of life. On my drive to work, I would catch myself crying about various things. For instance, I would think about my student's relationship with his parents and the next thing I knew I was crying about my dad. It had been almost ten years since his death and it was the oddest thing for me to get emotional about it now. Perhaps I was starting to let go of the anger and beginning to grieve.

The morning-drive crying sessions became more typical. It did not take much to make me cry about anything. I kept asking myself: *Why is this happening? Right now, everything is good and yet I am depressed and irritable!*

I realized I needed to speak to a psychiatrist on a consistent basis. My interrupted sleep was definitely becoming a problem.

October 2003

I got through a month of school unscathed. It was my first time teaching both girls and boys. I felt happy that within a month I was already developing a relationship with my students.

I had become more observant since high school days, and my students came from homes similar to those I once knew. Yet, I experienced culture shock. At my previous job, most of the teachers were observant Jews. Here most were secular.

Earlier in the month, I'd seen the dermatologist for a quarterly check-up. She made sure to look at everything and take pictures of the moles that looked strange. Each time I visited, she measured them for changes in size or color. "Everything looks good," I remember her saying. I told her about a mole behind my knee that had been bothering me, one of the moles she had been watching carefully and, because it was causing me anxiety, she agreed to remove it. The minor procedure involved removing the whole lesion and required a few stitches. She said she would let me know the pathology results as soon as it was received. I sighed, more waiting.

The next week I called the office daily until finally, a week later, I got the results—dysplastic nevus. Doctors keep track of the dysplastic nevii moles because they have a good chance of developing into melanoma. My body makes a ton of those nevii. Ah! Thank God, this one was benign.

Tuesday, October 14

It was during the interim days of *Sukkoth*, "The Holiday of Booths," when we had school and one of the non-Jewish teachers said, "Oh, I think we're going to eat in the tent today." I laughed to myself because I realized how sheltered I had been over the past few years when I worked and lived in the same community where everyone was celebrating and eating in their *sukkahs*.

The school's *sukkah* was on the campus of its elementary school. The whole high school was bused over for lunch and after lunch a *hagigah* (celebration) followed with Jewish music. I felt a little awkward because it's hard to dance with students you hardly know. Nonetheless, I got into it.

On the way home I realized my right foot was hurting. I thought I must have strained it while dancing. I ignored it and figured the pain would eventually go away like all those sprained ankles of high school basketball days. It did not.

Wednesday, October 15

On my way home from work I got a call on my cell phone from Aunt Wilma, one of my mother's sisters, who had survived breast cancer. She told me everything was okay but that Aunt Gail, one of my mother's other sisters, had just come out of surgery—they had found breast cancer in her lymph nodes.

I was in shock. My Aunt Gail had first been diagnosed with breast cancer, which required a bilateral mastectomy, eleven years earlier. There was a chance of recurrence but, unfortunately, my aunt fell into that tenth percentile. No one had told me about it until now. Apparently she had felt a painful and swollen lymph node under her arm on Yom Kippur, October 6, and only told her immediate family about the surgery scheduled for nine days later.

I wanted to see Aunt Gail right away. I began crying on the phone. I asked my Aunt Wilma, "Is there something I can do? Can I come in and visit her?"

Aunt Wilma (trying to protect me) said, "Everything is okay. Maybe you should come into the city next week for a visit when you have more time." When I got off the phone I felt depressed and needed to do something.

I called Aunt Gail at home. She said she was feeling fine. I asked if I could come see her. She said she was all right—it wasn't necessary to drive into Manhattan. I explained that if she could manage, I needed to see for myself that she was really okay. I was scared and didn't want to put it off. I decided to bring little Marsha with me to cheer her up. When I got there I knew I had made the right decision.

My aunt really looked fine and told me she had put on lipstick for the occasion. I was very emotional—Marsha in my arms named for my mommy, Aunt Gail's late sister, who died of breast cancer, to cheer up my aunt who was experiencing her second bout with the same disease. I felt strong and glad that I had survived. My mother may have passed away but others lived on and I was one of them. We stayed a while and then I had to go home—but I was happy that I had followed my instincts and made the visit, if only for a short time.

During the drive home, I began to think about my aunt's cancer and realized I had never booked the Computed Axial Tomography (CAT) scan I was supposed to have scheduled. In addition, my foot was still bothering me from dancing at school the day before and, to my sudden horror, I realized the pain was coming from directly below the surgery site for my initial melanoma.

Friday, October 17

When I called my surgical oncologist to schedule a CAT scan his assistant informed me that the protocol had recently changed to include a Positron Emission Tomography (PET) scan. The surgical oncologist also happened to be a breast specialist. I told him about my aunt and then mentioned that my foot had been bothering me for the past few days.

"I know I am just being anxious about my aunt," I said nervously, looking for some affirmation and validation that everything was going to be okay.

Instead he replied, "I want you to come in and see me."

"I scheduled my CAT/PET scans for the following Friday and it would be nice to see you on the same day, considering I have to come into the city anyway," I said.

"No problem," he replied.

Before he hung up the phone, I said, "Maybe I'm just being silly about my foot. If the pain goes away in the next few days do I still have to come in? —I'm seeing you in November anyway."

"I want to see you," he said, "It will make me feel better." His response had the opposite effect on me.

Friday, October 24

The worst thing about cancer is not necessarily the testing. It's the waiting and not knowing that gets to me. The waiting would challenge even a person with normal patience, and by nature I tend to be impatient. I went to the city early for my PET/CAT scan and let the technicians know I felt pain in my foot. A few hours later, I met with my surgical oncologist at the hospital. As he examined my foot I asked, "What's the story?"

"It's either an infection or trauma to the bone because there isn't a lot of tissue left from where I performed the surgery," he said. After the exam I asked him when I would get my results from the PET/CAT scan.

"Why are you concerned? It's probably nothing."

"With all that's going on with my aunt, I haven't slept in a week."

Ten minutes later he called me back to his office. There was an "abnormality" on my right foot beneath the initial melanoma site but it did not appear on the scan as large as a typical melanoma. He also told me I had a cyst in my right ovary that I should follow-up with a pelvic ultrasound.

"*Great!*" I mumbled to myself.

He told me not to worry about the scan of my foot because, even though melanoma can spread to the bone, he had never seen it spread near the primary site. It usually travels through the bloodstream and lands on a bone or an organ in another part of the body. He asked me to get an X-ray. Since I was already in the city, I figured I might as well take care of it right away. I hurried back to the imaging place. After taking the X-rays, the technician told me to call my doctor on Monday for the results.

I'm not sure how I was feeling at that point, but I knew it was almost Shabbat and I had to get home. Luckily I made the train before Shabbat but, by the time I got to Lawrence, Shabbat had already started and so I walked home. I felt upset that I had to wait until Monday to hear the results.

Monday, October 27

The surgical oncologist called on my cell phone at work to say that the foot abnormality, which was located in the bone of the fourth metatarsal, showed up on the X-ray as well. Again he told me not to worry, but that he wanted one of his radiology colleagues to examine the X-ray more closely, and to expect his call.

Tuesday, October 28

The radiologist called on my way home from work. I missed my exit as he told me I needed to schedule both a magnetic resonance imaging (MRI) and an Aspiration Bone Biopsy of my fourth metatarsal. I tried to sound calm as I talked with this doctor but got lost in the circles around Kennedy Airport and the escalating, swirling worries going through my mind.

Wednesday, October 29

I had the MRI, which the radiologist explained would help him find the place in the bone to do the biopsy. My nervousness increased.

Thursday, October 30

I had the biopsy of the fourth metatarsal. It was not as uncomfortable as I had expected. I asked the radiologist when the results would be available.

"Your doctor will probably call you on Monday with the information."

Another weekend of waiting for information! How much patience is one person expected to have!

As the winter neared and the days got shorter, I realized that what had been my main concern just a few months earlier, the kids and our jobs, was not bothering me at all. Those concerns had been replaced with something worse—the fear of disease, the fear of death. And then I realized that in reality they were two aspects of the same worry—the fear of change, of the unknown—transition. I held my breath and waited and hoped that change would not come. I craved stability.

CHAPTER 3 - Late Fall 2003

Six Different Doctors in Six Different Offices of Six Different Hospitals

Josh

Doctors, I think I've seen enough of them lately! Yes, I know they do great things—but sometimes I feel they are better as hope agents than solution-bringers. They espouse science as fact, medicine as cure, and surgery as solution to those of us without their seven-year educational pasts and endless shifts they endured in the nightmare called medical training.

Maybe I'm jealous because that D-plus in Chem Lab 2 derailed my own medical aspirations. But I have nightmares too. It was a Wednesday in November, 2003, and did not start well. We're only a marathon's distance from most spots in Manhattan—but on this day we probably would have been better off had we left the car and run.

New York traffic has three levels: slow, bumper-to bumper, and parking lot, and we got the latter. Our nerves were already shot, and our patience low. But I digress. It was a throw-in to the day we met with six different doctors in six different offices of six different hospitals. Sure, someone might say that these hospitals were connected; but when I have to get in another taxi or bus or subway or shuttle or walk a mile to get to the next appointment, that's different enough. Six doctors! And none of them had more clue than the next. When science does not work and medicine does not cure, what's left to do but to pray, pray, and pray for help from Somewhere Else?

Since there were so many Doctors — did I mention there were six? — I don't remember names, or even what they did specifically. I'm just left with my impressions that led me to give them nicknames:

Introducing…
Dr. Wizard-of-Pause: *the guy who kept telling us to be patient and "follow the yellow brick road," that things would work out. We listened until we realized that he was neither pulling any strings, nor did he have access to them.*

Dr. I-Can't-Help-You-But-I'll-Charge-You-for-it-Anyway: *Though something of a generic name considering the number of meetings today, this guy was particularly clueless about all things medical as well as interpersonal.*

The Ice Butcher: *I'm still not sure this guy was a doctor, but our experience with him alone was enough to give nightmares!*

Dr. Bowtie: *Memorable for nothing other than this clothing accessory, he confirmed that the medical profession was clueless about how to help us.*

The Professional: *By the time we got to his office my mind was so far gone, it didn't matter what he said. But Julie liked him.*

Dr. Six: *I could walk past this guy in the street, even though he was probably one of the most helpful doctors to us overall. I seriously have no idea, though, whether he was an oncologist or proctologist or dentist. Seriously, I was done.*

In the end, we found doctors who could offer help, as well as a path we could take even though it wasn't golden and yellow. And we owe an unpayable debt of gratitude to the doctors who did help us, and even those who tried and failed. They were trying to find solutions that in all fairness were not there.

The real nightmare is: medicine is not perfect. Human bodies don't always behave in predictable ways, their mysterious changes stumping even the most talented, brilliant and gifted doctors. Our bodies are wonders created by God, the source of life, endowed with unique processes that ebb and flow as the vessels that contain our souls. These souls connect us to each other, help us live and breathe, pray and hope.

Had all the doctors we met that day been caring, soulful people, it would still have been a difficult blur of meetings, but not the nightmare it became. If they had become Agents of Hope and not only Problem Solvers, the six doctors might have helped solve problems, given comfort, and initiated coping with the difficult hours, days and months ahead.

Monday, November 2

Somebody once said, "It's not as bad as you think. It's worse." I have wondered about the wisdom of this type of negative language but I guess if taken in moderation it does give vent to complex feelings in difficult times.

I have learned from experience to prepare myself for the worst — I have also learned you can never fully prepare yourself — when I am about to hear bad news. If someone tells me, "I have some bad news," I immediately think — before I even get the news — of three worst-case scenarios to help cushion the blow. It's like the old Jewish telegram, "Start worrying — details to follow." That strategy failed me in the next few days.

My surgical oncologist called me at work to deliver the news: "You have a melanoma in the 4th metatarsal, the bone of the fourth toe. The reason you have been feeling pain in your foot is because the tumor is beginning to cause a fracture in the bone." I was speechless. He told me not to worry, that he had a friend who is an excellent plastic surgeon. He would try to get in touch with him and then get back to me. I hung up the phone, my mouth agape.

I began to process the doctor's words and realized that I had to ask him a question. Five minutes later, I called him back. "What does this mean? Tell me — what is the worst I can expect?"

"In all likelihood, the plastic surgeon will remove an inch or so of bone and patch it back." I let out a big sigh. I really trusted him and felt a great sense of relief.

Nevertheless, I knew I was going to need help to calm myself down. I did not realize it would take the strength of a village to help me — that doctors, therapists, medications, family, friends would all have to do their part just to get me to relax. The Serenity Prayer, which probably originated with Alcoholics Anonymous in the 1930s, reads:

> *God — Grant me the serenity to accept the things I cannot change, the courage to change the things I can, and the wisdom to know the difference.*

So I started on the goal of serenity. I looked in my wallet to find the phone numbers of psychiatrists whose names I had been given and made a call. One called me back immediately and an appointment was scheduled for the next day.

I was working on my courage at the same time as I tried to change my attitude to the current predicament. I got in touch with a healer who had helped me in the past. She practices Consegrity, a method of energy healing, and had treated me during the first melanoma. I figured it couldn't hurt to try. I then began looking for a massage therapist.

Though I had begun to work on serenity and courage, I wasn't sure which would be more beneficial to me and which would have the more important application to my condition. Would I have to accept my fate, the daughter of my mother's sad story? Or would I be able to choose a new ending to the story? I still did not have the wisdom to know the answer.

Tuesday, November 3

Today I met the new psychiatrist. He seems pleasant, maybe even compassionate. It felt difficult trying to develop a new relationship when he knew so little about me. He gave me some medication to help me sleep. God bless Ambien!

After meeting with the psychiatrist, I went for a pelvic ultrasound to check the cyst on my right ovary. Thank God, it was no longer there. The technician said I had probably been ovulating at the time of the PET/CAT Scan. I felt relieved because I was imagining the worst, as I am wont to do! I was preparing myself for both a total foot amputation and a hysterectomy. More "worst-case scenario" contingency planning!

Tuesday, November 4

I told my bosses about the anticipated surgery and that I would need three weeks off to recuperate which, at the time, would see me back at work on December 1, right after Thanksgiving.

Later that day I met my first medical oncologist, affiliated with the same hospital as my surgical oncologist. With the first melanoma I did not have an oncologist — the tumor had not spread to my lymph nodes even though it was classified as stage II. This time medical protocols demanded I see both the surgical oncologist and the dermatologist every three months — the former to monitor the lymph nodes on my right leg and the latter for full body checks.

Despite the need for follow-up appointments, I had thought I was done with this disease. Now that there was a recurrence and it was classified as a stage IV, I needed systemic treatment, a regime that would involve my whole body in case the disease spread further. Whereas I was not given any statistical information the first time around, now — even after the surgery — I had a 60 percent chance of another recurrence in my right foot, the primary site, and that did not include other potential melanomas that might appear on my body over time. It slowly began to dawn on me just how little doctors knew about this unpredictable and incurable disease.

The consultation with the medical oncologist was friendly, easygoing, and not too intimidating. The doctor told me about two options for post-surgical treatment: interferon treatment and Vaccine-Therapy. At that juncture, interferon was the only US Food and Drug Administration approved treatment for melanoma and Vaccine-Therapy was still undergoing clinical trials. The medical oncologist told me that most people opt for Vaccine-Therapy because it has very few side effects. The catch is that you need a certain blood type, HLA-A2 positive, which I later discovered I did not have. Consequently, I was not a candidate.

On the other hand, interferon was an invasive treatment that required a month of daily hour-and-half infusions and, for the subsequent eleven months, three shots a week. The two downsides were daunting. The first involved terrible side effects, such as chronic fatigue, flu-like symptoms and depression. *Great! I'm already depressed,* I thought to myself. The doctor said not to be concerned about the depression because she worked closely with psychiatrists throughout the treatment. *Wonderful,* was my cynical, unspoken reaction. I then learned of a man who was never depressed until he began interferon treatment, and who became suicidal.

The other downside was that the treatment only lowered my chances of recurrence by *8 percent*. That meant instead of having a 60 percent chance of recurrence, I would have all those nasty side effects only to lower my statistical probability of recurrence to 52 percent. It did not give me much hope but, at that point, it seemed all that was available and I began to consider it. I needed to do something to prevent this cancer from coming back.

I asked the doctor if I would be able to continue working during this treatment. She told me about a woman, also a teacher, who got her treatments at the end of her working day. The doctor explained that it left the woman with very little patience for her own children but at least she was able to continue working.

I started thinking up ways that would enable me to work while receiving treatment. I wanted to maintain everyday life as normal as possible. I worked across the street from North Shore University Hospital and figured someone must be there who could administer the treatment.

At the end of meeting the medical oncologist, my sister asked the doctor a question: "Is it possible that more than a piece of her fourth metatarsal would need to be removed?"

I got angry and immediately shot back at her with a little too much confidence, "My surgical oncologist has already said they no longer perform amputations on melanoma patients." I could not believe my sister would suggest such a thing! The oncologist did not respond and my sister was silent. We thanked the doctor for her time, and left.

Wednesday, November 5

I took the day off because I had appointments in Manhattan.

We had to get to the plastic surgeon's office by 9:30 AM but, with the heavy traffic that morning, Josh and I were in the car for two hours and ended up being a half hour late. My Aunt Wilma, who was meeting us there, had already spoken to the plastic surgeon so by the time we arrived he knew the details and told me he could not help me. The situation was "beyond my expertise," he said and he recommended an orthopedist instead.

The plastic surgeon explained to the three of us that he had received all the slides and materials the day before and knew then that he couldn't help us. I started to get angry and if you know me, it takes a lot to get me to yell.

"If you had all this information yesterday couldn't you have saved us the trip of coming into the city?"

I was frustrated. The prospect of the appointment had given me hope that this doctor would be able to help me. My aunt went into damage control by apologizing on my behalf and thanking him for his time.

As we were leaving the office, the assistant had the audacity to give me a bill for $175 because they do not accept insurance.

I showed Josh the bill and said, "Now you know why plastic surgeons do so well—you have to pay them even if they know they can't help you!" I guess I spoke too loudly because, immediately, another woman came from behind the desk and voided my credit card charge. I would have paid it, but it was both appropriate and courteous that she should void the charge. However, as an ironic postscript to this farce, I later received a receipt from my insurance company, which confirmed that the doctor did, in fact, bill them for the entire consultation fee.

Our next appointment was not until the afternoon. As we walked out of the plastic surgeon's office, my surgical oncologist met us and escorted us back to his office. He apologized that his plastic surgeon colleague was unable to help but said that he had scheduled an appointment with the orthopedist (who had been recommended by the plastic surgeon), in half an hour. The surgical oncologist told us he had never met this orthopedist but that he trusted the plastic surgeon to make a good recommendation.

Now, this would have been a good time for my surgical oncologist to inform me that my condition was worse than what he had prepared me for—but he did not. As far as I knew then, I would need a minor procedure to remove an inch of my fourth toe and then some Vaccine Therapy to boost my immune system.

Two of my brothers-in-law are doctors. The previous night I had spoken to them about the upcoming appointments. My sister Deborah is married to Marc and Josh's sister Leora is married to Michael. Both men tried to caution me that the removal might be more than an inch, and might even include the entire fourth metatarsal. Both seemed to think the toe could easily be replaced with some kind of pin implanted in my foot.

Yet, back at the surgical oncologist's office he still had not mentioned the possibility of a procedure of such severity and in a laid back way advised, "Just see the orthopedist and hear what he has to say, then we'll talk." He also knew I was going to a different hospital that day for a second opinion about my case. He then said jokingly, "Oh, you're going to the *bowtie* hospital," a reference to the competition between New York's two major cancer centers.

The orthopedist's office was only a block away. By the time we got there, my sister Deborah had joined us. The orthopedist had a cold disposition. Marc had already warned me that, "you choose a surgeon based on skill, not on personality." I tried to put my initial judgment behind me and, realizing he was an Israeli, I tried to make small talk in Hebrew but to no avail. He was only interested in seeing the X-rays, PET scans and MRIs.

He shuffled through all my paperwork, huffing and sighing that it should be more organized, until he found the X-ray he was looking for. He placed it on his board and lit it up. He began to show us where on my fourth metatarsal the tumor was located. He explained that it was dangerously close to the joint of the third metatarsal, putting it too at risk and pointed out that, since this was a recurrence, we needed to take this very seriously. I was carefully following him and understanding everything he said until he recommended "The Choppard."

"What is the Choppard?" I asked.

"It's the complete amputation of the foot right in front of the ankle bone."

Once again, I was in shock: I had not prepared for this.

"I was told that perhaps only an inch of the fourth metatarsal would need to be removed and at most, the entire metatarsal," I countered, struggling for words to defend my poor foot.

"This is a serious cancer and if you want my opinion, I would be more conservative," he replied coolly.

"Isn't there another option? What if we remove the third and fourth metatarsals and keep the first, second and fifth ones?"

He explained that the fifth toe cannot stand on its own without the third and the fourth to support it. However, he did make another suggestion.

"We could keep the first and second metatarsals and then remove the third, fourth, and fifth because that would still enable you to walk without a prosthetic."

I still hadn't completely absorbed all that he said, but I asked, "How soon could we schedule the surgery?" He left the room to check his calendar.

Once he had left the room, the tears began pouring down my face. Not only was I crying, but within seconds I must have used up a whole box of tissues. It was like a flashflood coming out of my body. Thank God, I had a Valium tablet with me that I took immediately. *I was not prepared for this!* I had asked my surgical oncologist over and over again if my foot would need to be removed, and he had stated, "No." I was in a state of shock. I felt frozen, caught in a time warp; completely out of control.

The doctor returned to the shocked group in his office. Despite seeing my face was bright red and swollen from tears, he offered no words of understanding or compassion. In a totally impassive manner, he gave me a date that was ten days away. We then told him that we were off to another hospital for a second opinion. His response was simply to shrug his shoulders as if the news was of no concern. Honestly, I think that my fear at the prospect of losing my foot was almost matched by my fear of this robotic-like doctor.

We took a taxi to the next hospital and the whole trip I was overwhelmed with convulsions of weeping. As I was going through the patient registration procedure, my surgical oncologist called me. Suddenly I was completely out of control, simultaneously yelling at him and crying over the phone, *"You did not prepare me for this! You told me I wasn't going to lose my foot!"* He kept trying to calm me down and said, "Let's just see what the second opinion will say."

I met the next surgical oncologist who had already reviewed my case by the time I entered his office. He, too, had never seen a melanoma metastasize to the bone beneath the initial site. This was not giving me much confidence in the expertise of the medical world, or in their prognosis of my condition. Nonetheless, he agreed that part of my foot would need to be amputated. He said the "Choppard" would not be necessary, "just" the removal of my third, fourth, and fifth toes. I actually felt relieved that at least I would have part of my foot.

"Do you work personally with an orthopedist?" I asked. Luckily the orthopedist who worked with this doctor happened to be available that day. Who would know that melanoma was such a big deal, with so many different doctors, protocols, treatments, and prognoses? I did not.

The surgical oncologist gave me the name of a medical oncologist and then I was off to see the orthopedic surgeon, my fifth doctor of the day. I met the orthopedist, and his manner immediately made me feel comfortable. *I can't believe it,* I said to myself, *he actually smiled!* I tried not to pass judgment based on his personality, but on skill alone, and failed miserably! Luckily, though, this doctor not only had an excellent manner with patients but also had experience with this type of surgery. He had just performed a "triple ray resection" — which in doctor's language means removal of the third, fourth, and fifth toes — on a diabetic woman who was now walking without an orthotic or prosthesis.

I quipped, "At least I'll be eligible for handicapped parking."

He immediately shot back at me with an emphatic, "*No*! You are going to walk again!"

His personality and experience with the procedure gave me more confidence than I had felt all day. I knew he was the doctor for me. I couldn't wait to call the other orthopedist to cancel the operation I had scheduled with him. In my head I referred to him as the "Butcher" or the "Chopper." The new orthopedist also agreed that a full amputation was much too aggressive and that the three ray resection would be aggressive enough. I liked him. He then explained that it would be his job to remove the cancer and the plastic surgeon's job to close up the wound. So, if by removing the cancer there might not be enough skin to close the wound, I would need a skin graft. Luckily for me this plastic surgeon was also available — my list of doctors attended that day now numbered six.

We waited a long time before meeting the plastic surgeon, who also had a very nice disposition and a gentle manner. Deborah and I drew pictures on my toes as jokes to remind the doctor which ones would need to go and which would need to stay. We also wrote a big "R" on my right foot just in case he had his left and right confused. The humor didn't bother me and the doctor smiled at it.

He explained his procedure in a similar way to that of the orthopedist. He also called me, "Jules," which is a nickname of endearment that only people close to me use. I said to him, "Do you know that you just called me Jules?" He laughed because he hadn't realized. It made me feel even more comfortable to learn that his wife's name is Julie.

By the time we left the hospital that day, my surgery was already scheduled: November 11. I had asked the orthopedist and the plastic surgeon when I could return to work, and they agreed that after Thanksgiving would be feasible even though I would not be able to put full pressure on my foot. To me, that was good enough news.

Thursday, November 6

I went back to work happy because I knew I would need only three weeks off, and if I could arrange my interferon treatment at North Shore Hospital everything would be as normal as possible. Yes, I knew I had cancer in my foot and yes, I knew that part of that foot would need to be removed but I yearned for the return to normalcy.

Now was the strong and hopeful feeling that this melanoma would not be a major obstacle in my life.

However, by this time my anxiety level was increasing and my sleep was getting worse. My psychiatrist raised the dosage of Prozac and Klonopin and gave me a different medication for staying asleep, which was my new problem. My Consegrity therapist suggested that, when I could not sleep, I should work on rhythmic breathing. I tried to take deep breaths but was too anxious to calm down so I relied on the medicine to do the job.

I took advantage of the moment and decided to allow myself massages at home, which made me feel so relaxed that I scheduled them twice a week. Though I felt guilty about indulging myself, I also thought I should do "whatever it takes."

Despite all this, as my surgery date grew closer I simply could not stop crying. Every time I looked at my children I began to cry in fear and guilt that I would put them through what I had been through. I was scared that I was going to die and every time I thought about it or looked at one of the kids I burst into tears.

My sister Caroline flew in from Los Angeles for the surgery. Caroline, Deborah, and I decided to arrange a "girls" weekend away to distract me from the upcoming surgery. Josh seemed supportive but I could tell he was nervous. I tried to reassure him I was not distancing myself intentionally, as my mother had done to protect her children. I sensed that Josh thought I was doing the same thing, preparing for death. Maybe so, but if I didn't go I would be crying the entire weekend. He eventually said I was distancing myself from my children. This was hard to hear and hard to accept. In my mind, it had nothing to do with him or how I felt about our children. I was exhausted, in pain, and emotionally drained.

Friday, November 7

Road Trip! I scheduled spa treatments for everyone and was looking forward to the weekend. During the drive we made foot jokes: *Maybe you should get a thirty percent discount on pedicures now that you're losing three toes!* Yes, the humor was dark but I was laughing instead of crying.

We arrived at the inn and they put us in one room for Friday night and another for Saturday night. I spoke to the man at the desk and could not believe the words that came out of my mouth. I said, "I have cancer. This is my last weekend before surgery and we all came here to get away. Do you think you could look in your computer again and see if anything else is available?"

The man said he knew what I was going through because his father had colon cancer and things weren't fun in his house either. Guess what? We got a duplex, two bedroom apartment and we could all stay together. Everyone was laughing at me that I used the cancer line, but it was all true. We had come to relax and get away. Sometimes it doesn't hurt to tell the truth.

Sunday, November 9

By the time I got home Sunday evening the children were already sleeping. I felt bad to have missed another day with them, but I had a great time over the weekend. Had I not been diagnosed with cancer, we would never have gone away. Josh's mother had arrived prior to the weekend so Josh didn't have the entire burden of our kids. I thanked him many times and told him how badly I had needed that weekend. He said he felt good that I had enjoyed myself but I think he felt better just to have me home.

Monday, November 10

I don't remember much about the day before my surgery except for speaking to Zach and Ozzie's teachers about my condition and telling them to expect some changes in behavior and signs of anxiety. Both teachers gave assurances that they would watch out for anything irregular, give our kids extra hugs, and take care of them.

I was nervous about the surgery and worried for my children and my husband if something were to happen to me. I thought of writing a letter to each child, just in case something went wrong, to let them know their mother loves them. I felt like a soldier going to war, writing a last letter to my family members. Josh tried to boost my confidence that I would return home. I tried to explain to him my fear. "They are so young. How will they remember that I loved them?"

Instead, I wrote Josh a letter. This is an excerpt:

My Dearest Josh,

…I know you must be scared. I am terrified. I never imagined that life could be this good in spite of my previous traumas. So what I ask of you tomorrow is not just to pray for me or for yourself, but to pray for us.

… I believe that love is the greatest healer. We have worked too hard to surrender. Our love for each other, for our children, must continue to shine….

Please do not despair. This is just one more of the many hurdles to come. We'll get better at them as long as we believe that we can jump…. The moment the hurdle feels too high, the faster we will trip and fall. I believe that we will get through this, but I want and need you to have faith too. It is all in our perception of reality. We are the agents and there are some things that are within our control…. It's not over; it's just another detour along the long highway of life.

Believe in me, believe in us, and most importantly, believe in yourself.

My love to you forever,

Julie.

I gave Josh the letter and as he read it he began to cry. I went to find a safety pin. I pricked my finger and even though Josh is terrified of needles he gave me his hand and let me prick his. I accidentally pushed too far and he let out a yelp and we laughed through our tears. We held our pricked fingers together as a sign that we are inseparable and that we are of the same blood. It would be that blood that would keep us together.

We cried, we hugged, and then we both took something to help us sleep and turned off the lights.

CHAPTER 4 – Surgery and Post-Op
Waiting Rooms

Hurry up so we can wait. — *Anonymous*

Josh

Waiting rooms; Rows of not quite comfortable chairs with soft pastel colors line the walls and form a row back-to-back down the middle. Small tables hold week-old magazines with month-old information. I watch other people. I know I'm trying to get into their heads — am I stealing? A large squat middle-aged woman in the corner, snoring. How long has she been here? Candy wrappers, half-eaten bags of potato chips and pretzels come from the vending machines twelve floors and two wings away. In the background, someone changes the television channel and tunes into the shriek of a woman who just realized that her brother is really her long lost stepson's evil twin who married her sister, in the dramatic finale of the longest running soap opera. At least she didn't have cancer.

There's relief in knowing you're not the only one waiting on pins and needles for a loved one to get good results. But are there good results in the cancer ward waiting room?

A girl walks by with "Cancer Sucks" emblazoned on her tee-shirt. She can't be more than 14 or 15, but looks older with the do-rag wrapped around a bald head, familiar to most everyone in the room. As she's about to flow out of the room and out of our lives, an old lady stops her, and asks, "Where'dya get that great shirt, hon?"

There's always a flow in a waiting room. New people come in; occasionally one of the midnight warriors get up and trek to the restroom, vending machines or cafeteria. On occasion a nurse — or worse, a resident — or worst, a real doctor — comes to bring them to see their loved one and discuss treatment, surgery, options, diagnoses, prognoses, death, life, and the need to return for more tests — the purgatorial dreams of childhood.

People get up, stretch, ask their new-found friends from the Waiting Room Gang to watch their stuff, hold their seat — and is there anything they could get you on their adventure? — A soda? — Chocolate bar? — Anything to remind you that a world exists beyond these four pastel colored walls of the Waiting Room?

Now I try to be philosophical about it. I ponder the Waiting Room of Life — yeah, my life has become a waiting room.

Tuesday, November 11

The day of my surgery, only Zach understood what was going on. He remembered my crutches after Marsha's birth and occasionally asked, "When is your foot going to get better?" Up to this point I had told him that, despite the scar, my foot was better. Now I had to tell him my foot had gotten sick again and I would need to go back to the hospital for a few days. He said, "Mom, I'm going to come and visit you like I did last time." Tears welled in my eyes because he was confusing this hospital stay with his visit to me in the hospital — when Marsha was born. He hadn't come to visit on the day of my first surgery. At that time, even though I was entitled to spend the night, I chose not to because I so badly wanted to go home to my family. Nine days earlier I had spent five days in the hospital with the new-born Marsha. I missed my boys, and I missed my baby.

Josh drove me into the city. My mother's three sisters — Aunt Wilma, Aunt Gail, and Aunt Sharon, along with my sisters Caroline and Deborah and my brother, Douglas, and his wife Pamela — met us at the hospital. My mother-in-law, Norma, wanted to be there, but we asked her to be at home with our kids instead. When we got there the nurse said my surgery had been delayed and asked if we wanted to go upstairs to the art room while we waited. My aunts and sisters got excited about the prospect of creating art projects but, for me, art had always been frustrating — especially today. I had trouble making a picture frame that my son could have easily made in preschool. The delay and the so-called artistic opportunity irritated me.

Finally I was called for surgery. Josh and my sisters brought me to another waiting area. We again drew pictures on my foot to give the doctor directions. The chaplain of the hospital came by, as did several nurses. Finally, I said goodbye and was wheeled into the Operating Room.

The next thing I remember is waking up from anesthesia and crying that I wanted my husband. The doctor calmly tried to explain that I was in recovery and would see my family soon. I cried. I started screaming, "*I need to see my husband right now!*" I didn't know it but Josh and my sisters were outside the ward, pleading with the nurses to let them in.

Between the disturbances I was causing and my husband's cajoling, something clicked and, contrary to regulations, the doctor allowed Josh to slip into the recovery room. When I saw Josh I just grabbed on to him and held tight, as I never had before. I had been so scared that I wouldn't wake up from the surgery that I needed his big arms to envelop me and assure me that he wouldn't let go. All along I had been concerned about leaving him and now I didn't want him to leave me.

I must have passed out again and awoke to find myself in a pleasant private room. My sisters had told me that the cancer floor would make me feel uncomfortable and — well, sick. So they found a private room that felt like a five-star hotel, sans Jacuzzi. I appreciated the private room, but I wanted to be among other cancer patients, to identify with other patients, otherwise I felt it was as if this private room meant: *We're not really dealing with cancer inside a cancer hospital.* In the end, it was for the best, and I didn't realize how difficult it might have been.

Friday, November 14

My four days in the hospital were all a blur. I don't remember the difference between night and day. I don't remember eating anything. I do remember images of people who came to visit me but the nurses kept me drugged to numb the pain so that everything seemed surreal.

I was supposed to be discharged on Friday but I just was not ready to go home yet. I suggested to Deborah that Caroline and I could stay with her for Shabbat and she agreed. Douglas and Pamela came over Friday night for dinner and it was a very pleasant, quiet meal. I needed that one more day before I returned home to my family, to reality.

Saturday, November 15

Josh picked me up after Shabbat, on Saturday night, and we returned home. The kids were already sleeping by the time we arrived and my mother-in-law, Norma, was standing by the front door waiting for us. She had been watching over the kids while I was in the hospital. Norma is a professor at a university in Montreal and it was lucky for us that my surgery and recuperation coincided with her academic vacation. I took some painkillers, went straight to bed, and passed out.

Sunday, November 17

There is a memory of briefly seeing my children, but I spent most of the day in bed and felt like a shadow on the wall.

Thursday, November 19

I had a meeting with the medical oncologist affiliated with the hospital where the surgery was performed. She smirked when we told her the previous medical oncologist had recommended interferon and said I needed a more aggressive treatment to prevent a recurrence. She suggested the protocol of Thalidomide and Timidor, a form of chemotherapy. Since the tumor had spread to the bone there may be some cancer cells already in my bloodstream. I needed a systemic treatment that would kill those cells. Interferon, a form of immunotherapy, only strengthens the immune system to prevent recurrences and cannot eliminate cancer cells already present in the body.

I liked what she had to say because she was offering me something more aggressive. It felt as though I was being proactive and responsible in handling my disease, exhibiting the courage to change the things I can. The child of a sick mother now becomes the sick mom; I had to do whatever I could to stay alive even if that meant some difficult months with chemotherapy. This medical oncologist seemed to be offering something tangible even though it was still in the clinical trial phase.

Nonetheless we tried to suspend our judgment until we met another doctor at Marc's initiative. He had been the head of the melanoma department where my surgical oncologist worked, but now led the Cancer Center at a different hospital. As there was no clear path of treatment that offered me a cure, Marc thought this doctor could provide objectivity in determining which treatment to choose. He helped us map out all our options. The first choice was to do nothing because at the moment I was cancer-free. Though, considering my chances of a recurrence, he did not advise following this course. At his office it was finally spelled out to me what would happen in the event of a further recurrence: *It could cost me my life*. If this melanoma returned there was no guarantee it would not attack my internal organs. There is no cure for such metastasis, only continuing clinical trials.

We discussed the interferon option as well as the chemotherapy option. The doctor didn't like the latter because melanoma cells are not generally responsive to chemotherapy. We decided to put the Vaccine Therapy on hold as, perhaps, something to do after the initial treatment. He told us that sometimes there are vaccines available to people who are not HLA-A2 positive. His only real recommendation for us was something we had already planned — to go to Philadelphia and meet with a renowned melanoma specialist who would map out more options for me.

My appointment in Philadelphia was a week away. There was no way I was going to wait until then to hear about more options! I began scanning the Internet looking for clinical trials and other treatment options.

A well-known woman in the Orthodox community called me out of the blue and suggested I get in touch with a rabbi in Israel who is aware of all the top medical specialists in the world and their latest treatments. He gave me the name of a doctor in Texas who was treating late stages of melanoma with something called Biochemotherapy. Until recently this treatment had been used exclusively for people with stage IV metastatic melanoma and only a few months to live.

I later spoke with a man who was treated by this doctor. He had an inoperable melanoma tumor in his lung and no one wanted to treat him. He went through the treatment for seven rounds and the tumor shrunk to nothing. Two years later the tumor returned but, because he was under careful supervision, it was removed.

I called the doctor in Texas and he said I was a good candidate for his protocol, considering I was stage IV and cancer-free, but an adjuvant or accompanying treatment was necessary to prevent recurrences. From his perspective, without a systemic treatment I was only cancer-free for the moment.

The Biochemotherapy suggested by the doctor was serious stuff. It was a five-day in-patient treatment followed by fourteen days at home or in a hotel until the next round of treatment. I would need to go to Houston for three rounds. In fact, the doctor required all of his patients to stay in Houston for the first six weeks so he could monitor them. There were concerns that a low white-blood-cell count, a low platelet count, or even a virus when on this treatment would require hospitalization. The treatment consisted of three chemotherapy drugs: D.T.I.C., Cisplatin, Vineblastine and two immunotherapy drugs, interferon and Interleukin II. It was a highly toxic "cocktail" with many difficult side effects.

I decided that this was the treatment I needed. Though highly aggressive, I felt this was the best choice since I am young with a loving husband and three young children to help fuel the courage to change my fate.

Before even discussing this with Josh, I began to get anxious and depressed. Who would go with me? I couldn't stay in a hotel by myself. Who was going to take care of our children if I needed Josh to come to Houston? I didn't know what to do. On one hand, there was a chance that this treatment could save my life but, on the other hand, the thought of leaving the kids with a babysitter for such a long period of time made me nauseous. I decided to put off making a decision until we went to Philadelphia to meet the other doctor.

In the interim I got good news: all the margins on my foot where the operation had been were clear!

Friday, November 20

The following day I had a check-up with the plastic surgeon and the orthopedist. It had been almost two weeks since the surgery, but my stitches were still not ready to come out. I was frustrated. I was eager to heal and learn how to walk again, but had been told not to bear any weight on the foot—and that included driving. It made me feel incapacitated and dependent.

That evening the man in our community responsible for cemetery burials came to our home for me to sign papers that would release my foot from the hospital to be buried in a Jewish cemetery. It was odd seeing all the cemetery plots my family had. There was a space next to my mother, but I felt awkward taking it even though my father had chosen to be buried in Israel. At least we would somehow be connected, but how? Was I to be the heiress to my mother's shortened life and experience? I still didn't know, so I chose the plot not to the right of her, but beneath her. Close, but not the same.

Monday, November 24

I saw my psychiatrist and couldn't stop crying about the possibility that I might have to leave my children for six weeks as well as find someone to take care of them. I was scared I was becoming my mother—going away for long stretches of time, hiring people—maybe the wrong people—to care for my kids. My psychiatrist tried to calm me down. "Right now you need to focus on your own health even if it means being far away from the kids. Perhaps they could visit you." It was a hard day and not much could be said that would console me.

Then all of a sudden I realized it was Josh's birthday and I had totally forgotten! I felt terrible. Usually I get the kids to bake a cake, but I felt bad that I just threw it on them and that we didn't have the time to prepare for "Daddy's" party. Zach was fine with it except he wanted to go to the toy store to buy Josh a gift.

It occurred to me that it might be a nice idea to take Josh to Atlantic City on the way to Philadelphia, and we were going there the following day anyway. I suggested that we leave after the kids went to bed and celebrate his birthday at a new resort. We reached the hotel at 11:30 pm and passed out.

Tuesday, November 25

The next morning, as we sat at the Blackjack table, an older man came to sit down in the empty seat next to Josh. He looked at me and at my foot, which was in a bootie, and noticed the crutches. He asked me what happened and I told him I had some surgery. He asked why I needed the surgery. So I told him about the melanoma and that we were on our way to Philadelphia to see a doctor. The man said he had pancreatic cancer (another incurable one) and had joined a clinical trial that was treating with interferon. He was one of twenty who participated in the clinical trial and the only one who survived. He said they called him the "miracle patient." I thought, *I guess the trial wasn't so successful.*

Meanwhile Josh was trying to ignore our conversation but could not because he was losing at Blackjack round after round! The man put his arm around Josh's shoulder and said, "Don't worry; it's all going to be okay." I had a dollar out to tip the waitress for a drink; the man handed me a one dollar chip and said, "The drink is on me."

He said the chip is for good luck. I gave him my thanks and have been carrying that chip in my pocket ever since. He must have been an angel sent to tell us everything would be all right. Months later when I was able to let go of the one dollar chip, I bet it on a Blackjack round and won.

Later that day we arrived at the hospital. The doctor said, "You're a candidate for Biochemotherapy."

I had thought they only did that in Texas. The doctor said she had been giving Biochemotherapy to patients with stage III/IV resected melanoma. I became excited. "You mean I can go home after the week of treatment until the next round?"

Going home might risk exposure to viruses, but she said we would talk about it and, being two hours away from New York, the kids could come and visit me. I felt relieved. The day before I had thought I would have to say goodbye to my kids for six weeks. This was a better option.

On the drive home I realized my hope of returning to work on December 1 was not realistic. I could not start the Biochemo until after my foot was completely healed. That meant more time at home resting my foot, but anyone who knows me also knows I cannot rest until exhaustion sets in.

If I could no longer teach, who was I? I felt scared and lost. Up until now I had been convincing myself and everyone else I would be back at work after Thanksgiving. I decided to call, from the car, a school psychologist with whom I had developed a relationship during my two months at the job. I told her how the treatment would disable me. I wanted her advice as to how I should tell the principal and perhaps save my job. She asked me to let her speak to him first and later that day called back to advise me they would come to my house that evening to talk.

Later that evening, after our return from Philadelphia, the principal and the school psychologist came over. I was already crying when I told him I had to take a longer leave and that perhaps, if all was well, I would return to work in April. He was quiet. I said to him, "I realize I am new to your staff and that you will probably say, "Call me in April and we'll see what positions are available for the next year." I only had a one-year contract.

He said, "Forget about April. Get yourself better and you'll come back in September."

The assurance of a job for next year was the greatest gift he could have given. I asked, "If I'm feeling better, could I use the library to prepare next year's courses?"

Laughing, he said, "Come whenever you want. You have your security card. Move into the library for all I care. We want to let you know that your job is not going to be one of your worries. We asked you to work here and we will wait and look forward to your coming back."

If my foot had not been wrapped in bandages, I would have jumped for joy.

I was grateful to have at least been able to work for two months at my new job. Despite fears that I would not find the camaraderie I had enjoyed with previous colleagues, I was pleasantly surprised at how quickly I was absorbed into the new faculty. When I returned to school for a visit, in between my foot surgery and the start of Biochemotherapy, I was greeted by so many happy faces of students and faculty that I really felt they had missed me. Others sent get-well cards. Students I had not even taught stopped me in the hallway and asked how I was doing. Yet, I question what I had done to deserve their thoughts and prayers and feel guilty that I don't do enough for others.

Wednesday, November 26

Everyone who has seen me over the past few days has said I look more relaxed. I have more patience with my children and life at home is slowly returning to normal. It definitely helps to have a chosen a treatment, a location, and set a date for it to begin. Now the Thanksgiving weekend would give us some good down time. Instead of whining, Zach and Ozzie were laughing and being silly with their daddy. We were all happier.

Zach, with whom I usually initiate hugs, kept asking me all day if he could hug and kiss me. My heart swelled with warmth. I had been worried that whatever trauma he had experienced from my surgery might have been irreparable. Letting me know in his own way how much he loved me made me feel better.

CHAPTER 5 – Recuperation & Support

Who Will Take Care of the Kids?

Josh

Eventually, all of these factors helped me realize that I needed to become a Super Dad. But one night in particular, after Julie had been diagnosed the first time with cancer but before Marsha was born, helped solidify it.

It all started out well enough. Julie left at 5:30 AM, even though her event didn't start until 6:30 AM — oh well, I guess she had a hard day. And then there was the cancer lurking in the background. It had not hit us yet, but we knew it was there.

Anyway, so there I was: Zach hadn't eaten, both boys needed a bath — just an hour and a half, maybe two, away from the finish line: bedtime. And like I said: it started easy enough. Ozzie sat in his chair munching on one of Zach's French fries and making enough noise for his big brother to see that the little guy was eating his food.

"That's my French fry!"

"You better come and eat it before Ozzie eats them all."

Sizing the little big man up, Zach probably realized that Ozzie had the potential to do that very thing, so he quickly hopped up into his chair to eat.

As Zach finished his last fry, with some help from a starving dad, I asked: "Who wants a bath?"

"Dadadadee," said the little guy.

"I want to put colors in the bath," said Zach, referring to the paint pellets that he recently got as a gift for his birthday. And yes: isn't he using his words nicely? Then the phone rings. It's my brother. I tell him I have my hands full and have to go.

I go back and try to put them in again. The doorbell rings and it's the delivery people bringing in a table and mirror Julie ordered. "Remember to tip them a few bucks," she had said before she left.

Finally, I got Ozzie and Zach into the black or very dark blue bath tub filled with non-permanent coloring and water.

There are two approaches to bath time. Some parents like to get the kids in and out as fast as possible for several reasons. First, it may be dangerous because a kid can drown, slip, swallow too much water, etc. Second, a parent runs the risk of getting soaked.

The other philosophy of bath time is — milk it, baby, milk it. This is my philosophy on the matter, and I'll tell you why. You have two kids who generally want to be in different rooms doing different things; but here they have a limited range of motion — especially the one strapped in a chair. They keep themselves busy for the most part: no need for the "daddy toy" to be on full power. So, I let them stay in the tub a little longer than usual.

However, during their play time in the tub, Ozzie bounded into the soap dish.

"Whaaaaaaaaaaaaaaaaaaa!" And that was just me! You should have heard the lungs on this kid. I reached for his towel to take him out. But it wasn't there. It wasn't in his room on his laundry basket where it usually is, either. So, I grabbed him to me, hugged him — and, of course, got a little wetter in the process.

Zach was now as happy as a pea in a pod so I left him in the bath and ran to look for Ozzie's towel. By now he had calmed down and was casually sucking his thumb. I, of course, was a little more wet..., but certainly more concerned about my son's face. I thought, "If Julie comes home and sees a black and blue mark, I am going to get killed!" And, it goes without saying that I didn't want the little bugger to be hurt or physically marred or anything like that either.

Miraculously, there were no marks anywhere to be seen on the kid's face. Phew! I'm okay... uh, I mean, he's okay, I thought to myself. But there's something I'm forgetting... Oops! Zach was still in the tub. And any good parent knows you don't leave your kid in the tub all alone. If you don't know why see the first approach to bath time outlined above. Anyway, the kid was okay despite the prunes his fingers had become. I helped him out of the tub.

"I have to make a pee-pee in the potty," he said. I'm so proud. While holding Ozzie I helped him into the seat and sort-of watched him go, though I wish I would have watched more carefully.

"All finished," he said as he jumped down, flushed the toilet and climbed on the sink to wash his hands. Did I say I was proud?

I'd like to pause here. How many times do we look back at a situation and say, "If only..."? At this point it was 6:40 AM. Life was good. I was an innocent. I would survive. And then, all of the sudden, the dam cracked. As I tried to get the pull-up on him, Zach was able to wriggle away. Had it been a regular diaper, would he have been successful? We'll never know.

He walked over slowly, Ozzie watching — and probably learning every move — and then said "I have to go," and ran out of the room and into his own. I grabbed Ozzie and went to play with them in Zach's room.

"I want to get under the covers," said my naked-just-turned-three-not-fully-potty-trained son. Not an abnormal move for him, he slid under the covers and giggled. And then the evening got ugly.

"I have to make a pee-pee on the potty," he said. So I went to lift the covers.

"Don't go yet....," WOOOOOSHH! Had someone walked in a moment later — as I wish you had, honey — they would have thought I had wet myself. Zach's aim was perfect: he hit my inner thigh on a line drive. For those of us who've experienced being urinated on several times, this may not seem like such a big deal. But the first time is rough.

"It's mostly water, it's mostly water," I told myself. I told Ozzie to stay (ha!) and I told Zach that it was alright, don't step in it, no I mean it, no don't, a few times and took him to finish the job in the bathroom. He complied, flushed, and washed.

Upon returning to his room, I realized that Ozzie had climbed on to Zach's bed because he saw the chance to play with his big brother's treasured monkey with no one around — an understandable failing on his behalf, though unfortunately he ended up sitting right smack-dab in the middle of Zach's puddle of urine. I grabbed him off the bed, gave Zach the monkey and began to strip the bed.

Ozzie started to cry because I took the monkey away from him. Zach started to cry because I was stripping his precious bed. And I was on the verge.

What a picture! Here we were, the three Joseph men, covered in pee all of us, tears running down our cheeks. Wow, what a bonding moment.

I stripped the bed while the boys cried. The problem was that the bed itself was wet. Where to get a bed? Downstairs! So, I put Ozzie in his room –out of trouble (ha!) — grabbed the mattress and wet sheets and ran down to the basement. I stick the sheets in the laundry room, grab the extra mattress, with mattress cover still attached, and run upstairs. Ozzie had managed in the 45 seconds I was downstairs to grab his blanket off his crib and drag it into what had been a closed bathroom door, and he was now attempting to get back into the bathtub with it.

Zach was nearly hysterical, wailing for his mother while I silently prayed she actually would hear him using some sort of feminine, motherly intuition super-hearing. It wasn't to be. The sobbing continued until the first sheet was on, and gradually the tears turned into smiles as his bed became good as new. This time I got him into his pajamas and pull-up. And he got under the covers.

Meanwhile, Ozzie enjoyed the whole thing and was smiling as I picked him up, and everything was calming down when I realized he was still sopping wet. So, I got out a fresh onesie and new pajamas and again things started to calm down when he started to wail.

As he continued to wail, Zach informed me that he was tired, and wanted to go to sleep and needed his chocolate milk right away. I convinced him that room service would arrive momentarily but that

I needed to give Ozzie a bottle first.

Then, another miracle occurred. A nearly-full bottle was sitting on the table next to Ozzie's bed. How old was it? It smelled good enough, there was enough in there, and the air-conditioner was on, so there was a chill in the room keeping it fresh…, or something like that.

Man, was he hungry. He sucked that thing down faster than you can say "got milk?" As he was finishing up, he turned to look at me with that look of "are you going to get me into that crib or what?" and I complied.

I got Zach his chocolate milk, read him a book, and the evening was finally over — until I really stepped in it. Poop that is. And not the thick pieces that you can easily maneuver around. No this was the sliding stuff, and by the time I realized that fact, I was on my way, head over heels down the steps. Where had it come from? At what point had it gotten there? Like the Loch Ness monster and the legend of Bigfoot, these questions might never be answered. Somehow, though, I managed to stifle my own yell of pain and anguish so as not to wake the kids, and that was all that really mattered.

Well, that's basically it. By the time I got done cleaning the house and myself, the key in the lock was turning and Julie was home. We're all lucky she was saved from the trauma of the evening, but, I know I'm probably a better dad for surviving that night.

Friday, November 28

There was still a major issue to be resolved: *Who was going to take care of the kids?* My mother-in-law was still with us and we were all racking our brains to figure out who could help us for three months.

I called a woman who used to take care of me when I was younger to see if she was available. She responded quickly that although she was not able to do it, maybe one of her students would be interested. Deborah called me later to tell me about a message she got from this former babysitter — she had freaked out.

"Why?" I asked. Deborah told me that when my mother was dying, this young woman had been about to enter college. My mother offered to pay her tuition if she would stay in New York and take care of us four children. At eighteen, this responsibility felt too weighty for her.

I guess she has always felt guilty about it. My asking her must have triggered something. Freaked out or not, I haven't heard back from her or her students since that first call.

So the search for an aide/mother's helper continued. I called agencies. Friends were asking friends for recommendations. That evening I held my first interview. It was Friday night, and Shabbat had already started for us, but that was the time she was available.

She seemed pleasant, but not what I was looking for. My mother-in-law agreed. I didn't need another babysitter. I needed someone who could help when I was vomiting, get the kids dressed for school, take them to their after school activities, take care of the grocery shopping, and pick up the dry cleaning. I needed a replacement for me.

After the interview, Josh, his brother Naph with fiancée Shanna, Norma, all three kids and I sat down at our Shabbat table. We began to sing *Shalom Aleichem,* a song that welcomes the Shabbat. I was so happy because it was one of the first Shabbatot in a while that started early enough for all three children to be awake and participate. Zach, Ozzie, and Marsha were clapping and singing. It was a moment of joy to see our children happy. It was as if they were singing, "Yeah! Our mommy's back!"

I burst into tears and left the room to go to the bathroom. The earlier interview, juxtaposed with the wonderful feeling of being surrounded by family, triggered a harsh memory — the crazy, abusive woman in whose care I was left after my mother died. Again I felt my destiny was becoming that of my mother. I was scared of inadvertently putting my children through the same pain I had experienced. A person may not be as he appears and neither my mother nor I had the luxury of time to find out. I wanted to protect my children from harm but felt out of control.

My mother had been 31 when she was diagnosed with breast cancer, only a few months after I was born. Thank God she lived five more years despite her terminal diagnosis. The family story is that she called me Julie because I was her jewel. Now I was the mother diagnosed with cancer at 29 years of age and 34 weeks pregnant with my baby girl. It's painful to think about, but Marsha will probably be our last child. Because the hormones activated in pregnancy might trigger a recurrence of the disease, pregnancy is not recommended for melanoma patients or cancer survivors. Though I would like to have more children, I would not risk my life to a have a fourth child if it meant leaving three children motherless.

Because I had grown up with a sick mother, I wouldn't allow myself to be sick—especially in front of my children. I only wanted to project strength. Then something strange happened on a Thursday at the end of July 2003—I started suffering from a bad headache. By the next day I was in so much pain that I cried like a baby, helplessly in front of my children. Luckily we had a neurologist in the neighborhood who quickly arranged for an EMT *Hatzalah* (Jewish sponsored ambulance corps) volunteer to come over and give me fluids. I was deteriorating and we were forced to go the hospital. Once there, they filled me with a mixture of painkillers and eventually I recovered and was eager to return home.

Our neighbor's daughters stayed at our house to watch the children as Josh and I got a lenient emergency ruling from our rabbi to travel to the hospital on Shabbat. I found out later the doctor had suspected spinal meningitis but it turned out to be my first migraine. We were also permitted to return home by taxi because our children were young and depended on our care.

Unfortunately the pain in my head slowly returned. Through that Shabbat, the neurologist and the Hatzalah volunteer kept me on intravenous fluids so I would not become dehydrated. It was not until evening that I felt the first signs of relief from the migraine.

That was the first time Josh and the children ever experienced my being sick. I mention this episode because as Josh and I prepared for my upcoming treatment, I reminded Josh how sick I had been back then—vomiting, and crying from pain. If he wanted to prepare himself for what I was about to go through it might help to think back to that first major migraine attack. I have had a few more migraines since then and Imitrex injections alleviate my symptoms. I just wonder if my body was warning me in July that something was about to go horribly wrong.

Sunday, November 30

I interviewed an aide who was recommended by a social worker. She was professional and seemed friendly to the children. I asked her a lot of hypothetical questions and made sure she knew this was a three-month position and that she was not permitted to change my children's eating and television habits.

One of the things I feared was that she might try to quiet the kids at times when I would need to rest. I would definitely need the rest, but have bad memories being told to play quietly because my mommy was resting or sleeping. I also tried to explain that I needed space and as I would become stronger she would have to back off and allow me some independence — the key to my survival spirit.

As I was talking to this woman it suddenly occurred to me that all the things I was telling her were things my mother-in-law already knew. Norma and I have a great relationship and she has learned how to help me and give me the space I need. And she loves our children. I began to wonder, *could she live with us for three months?* I did not know how to broach the topic because she has already reared her four children and gone back to school to finish her Ph.D. I have the utmost respect for Norma who has an active academic career that she takes very seriously, which is why I just assumed that she wouldn't be able to do it.

Josh and I spoke about it and we even ran the idea by Josh's sister, Leora, who also thought it would be appropriate to ask Norma to take leave for a semester. Josh said he had been thinking of asking her for some time, but wasn't sure how I would feel about it. I told him it was the ideal solution and would completely relieve me of anxieties and nightmares. Norma was the perfect choice; the only choice. She knew the kids' routines and knows and respects how Josh and I parent. As an added bonus, it would be good for Josh to have his mother around as personal support.

I said to Josh, "Let's talk to her, but you have to start." Leora was coaching us. We would have to make very clear to Norma that what we want and need is something only she could provide. Josh prefaced the conversation with his mother: we were going to talk and she was not allowed to interrupt or respond until the next day. Josh said

"Mum," as pronounced in Canada, "Mum, we need you. We have been tiptoeing around this idea and even interviewed people, but the bottom line is we are looking for another you." Without a moment's hesitation—let alone waiting the next day—Norma replied, "I had a feeling it was leading up to this. Not that I don't want to do it, but I have a lot of people depending upon me back in Montreal."

I started to cry and said, "I would have said something earlier, but didn't feel as though I had the right to ask because you are not my mother."

Norma answered, "Julie, my hesitance has nothing to do with the fact that you are my daughter-in-law. I love you as my own daughter and I think you know that. Okay, listen, I need to go back to Montreal and see if this could really work out. I'm going on Wednesday and I'll have to stay a week to sort out the details and meet with everyone in the department including the dean of the college." We all hugged and kissed goodnight and she promised to think more about it.

I realize now that we had no clue what was in store.

CHAPTER 6 – Winter 2003
Funky Mole and More Full Body Checks

Sunday, December 1

I have an appointment to see one of the nation's leading dermatologists, who happened to have worked with the doctor whose treatment I chose in Philadelphia. I took my book of medical photos that were taken of every mole on my body in 1998, the year Zachary was born, three years before my first melanoma diagnosis. I wanted to see him just to make sure my body was not making any other "funky" moles I should be concerned about.

I hate full body checks when the doctor says, "Now, lift your breasts please." The doctor is a melanoma and breast specialist. So every time I go to see him and he finishes looking at my right foot and checking the lymph nodes in my right leg, he gives me a breast examination. At this point I am already expecting him to ask, "Was your left breast always a little larger than your right one?" I blush and say," Yes." However, at my last visit the script changed slightly. He said, "Was your left breast always that droopy?" Once again, with my face turning hot, I replied, "Yes." I felt like telling him to write it in my chart already—"left droopy breast"—so he can save me the agony of future reminders.

Back at the dermatologist's office, he saw no "funky" moles. "Funky" is the politically correct word dermatologists use to describe weird looking moles—or perhaps they think it's funny and amusing. I watch out not only for recurrence of previous melanoma sites but also for new ones.

I had a few questions for the doctor. That day I had spoken with a melanoma survivor who suffered a number of recurrences. The conversation made me feel as though death was imminent. Later that afternoon, I spoke with a medical oncologist who was optimistic about my Biochemo treatment because the melanoma had not spread to my lymph nodes. So I asked the dermatologist, "How do I make sense of my condition?"

He answered, "You are somewhere in between. Yes, this is a serious and lethal disease but you have a good chance of fighting because it has not spread to your lymph nodes."

I then asked him whether there was anything I could do to prepare for this Biochemo—such as vitamins, teas, or certain foods. He told me that what I needed to do was keep living my life the way I had been living it, with a conscious attitude to eat healthy and wisely. He said something that I have often quoted since: "Having this reoccurrence is like having a ball hit between your eyes. Typically, you have to give yourself six months to get over the trauma of the diagnosis. In your case it might be a little longer because the Biochemo is a very difficult and toxic regimen. My advice to you is whatever makes Julie feel good you should do. If you like massages or taking baths—whatever it is—try to do the things that make you feel good."

His advice was very welcomed, especially because it validated one of my new hobbies, receiving massages. It also gave me permission to seek happiness even if people thought I was going too far. What this doctor was saying, as I interpreted it, was that my mental health was just as important as my physical health and I should use any strategy available to help me cope.

Tuesday, December 2

Norma is returning to Montreal today and will meet with the various faculty members to see if it's possible to take a leave of absence.

I made an appointment to meet with a child psychologist renowned in our neighborhood, and prepared a list of questions in readiness for our session:

1. How do we deal with my going away for a week each month?

2. Can Josh come with me or should he remain the stabilizing factor at home?

3. Having asked Josh's mom to help us out, was this a reasonable request?

4. Can I ask her even though I am a daughter-in-law and not her daughter?

5. As a child of a sick parent and now the sick parent, how do I avoid projecting anxieties onto my children?

6. How should we talk about the cancer with our children?

The psychologist responded:

"Regarding Josh coming to the hospital with you, it is only for one week. Your kids are young and don't have a real concept of time. As long as there is predictability as to when you are going and when you are coming back they will adjust."

"It is appropriate to ask Josh's mother to help because she is his mother and these are her grandchildren. You too, as a daughter-in-law, should feel entitled to ask — even though I understand it is difficult not having your parents."

"It's normal to feel anxious, especially as you are a child of a sick parent, but remember you are not your parents. Whatever you and Josh have provided for your children is already a different foundation than the one you received. So if something should happen to you, Josh is not like your father and you, as their mother, have already provided them with love, support, and stability. If you notice that your sons are becoming anxious and it is interfering with their everyday behavior then you should bring them in to talk to a child specialist. But the best thing to do is what you are already doing—being open and honest with your children. Kids are resilient and they can handle a lot."

The negative side of me spoke: "Look at me. I was once a resilient child. Now I have to deal with the effects of depression, anxiety, and cancer!"

The psychologist corrected me. "I meant they are resilient in the short term. Be open and aware of *their* issues, and they likely won't have *your* issues to deal with as adults. It sounds like you guys are well organized and prepared for what you have in store. May you have a full recovery and whatever I can do in the future please let me know."

I offered to pay him and he refused, saying "If you see me on a regular basis then we can talk about payment, but for today there is no charge."

What a special man, I thought to myself. I felt that meeting with him was important on many levels. It was important to hear we were doing the right things for our children and that our kind of open parenting is what could prevent them from carrying the burden of my wounds or the development of their own. I needed to hear that as a parent I was doing what I could to help my children, especially because I don't feel my siblings and I had any familial or psychological support after my mother's death. This is the theme of my life: correcting my parents' shortcomings. Because I lacked a strong role model for parenting I tend to doubt my ability. I see how others handle situations differently and begin to think, *maybe they are right.*

The strongest validation from this psychologist was that I was not crazy. Here I was organizing psychiatrists, psychologists, and social workers for me and my family, then talking things out with the directors and teachers at my kids' schools, and now we were seeing a child psychologist who could perhaps guide us on a path we might otherwise have missed. The best thing he could have said and did say was, "You guys are doing the right things and it sounds like you are really getting yourselves prepared for what is approaching."

Wednesday, December 3

I had not been to an obstetrician-gynecologist since my six weeks post-partum visit after Marsha's birth. As I waited in the examination room I began to cry because it was taking me back to a time I would have preferred to forget—when I was pregnant and had melanoma. As already mentioned, Marsha's birth was the perfect cover-up for any fear that might have been related to the first melanoma. Yet, just coming back to the office unleashed a watershed of tears.

The doctor walks in. She asks, "How is everything? How's the baby? How's the foot?" She knows about the recurrence and recommends that I have my ovaries removed—there may be a relationship between breast cancer and melanoma because *perhaps* they are both estrogen receptors. I have since found that the relationship between estrogen and Melanoma is merely a hypothesis. Yet, at the time, I thought to myself that this was the first I had heard of such a relationship. Then she recommended I undergo a colon screening because colon cancer might be related to breast and ovarian cancer, and concluded the consultation with "Everything looks good. Good luck with your treatment."

I left her office feeling pretty shaken up. I just had part of my foot amputated and now I need to consider the removal of my ovaries? I called my medical oncologist in Philadelphia and she said, "Eventually you can go for a colon screening, but it's not imperative that you do it now and in terms of removing any more of your body parts, let's get through Biochemo first."

I felt relieved and comforted by that conversation. First, she actually returned my phone call—which in my experience is not always typical of doctors—and second, she recognized that I am nervous and anxious, and was helpful in calming me down. I need a little hand-holding. This treatment I am trying to gear myself up for is scaring the daylights out of me.

Another positive note, Norma called to say that she had met with all the necessary people in her department and they support her coming to New York to help us out. One professor agreed to take on her obligation as chair of the department and another to cover a class she was scheduled to teach. But nothing would be final until her meeting with the dean the next day. The only thing that's holding me back from shouting hooray is that I had cancer, lost half of my foot, and await a brutal treatment. But yes, I am overjoyed.

Thursday, December 4

Josh drove me to my psychiatrist appointment because I was still unable to drive myself. Up until now he had been doing a great job in keeping it all together but, now that we had a lull between surgery and treatment, his own struggles were beginning to surface. I felt it was normal and just a matter of time before he would break. I too was depressed and my attitude was, *let's deal with it*.

I asked if Josh could join our session because I didn't feel like leaving him alone in the waiting room. He met my psychiatrist and we reviewed all the different professionals we had met with during the week. My psychiatrist said, "It sounds like you guys are gearing up for a battle. It is a battle, and you are getting yourselves prepared. For other people it doesn't always hit them this early to prepare, so what you are doing is good."

Yes, validation is good to hear and the battle metaphor was helpful and accurate. In fact, months later I will ask people to call me by my Hebrew name, *Yael*. Yael was a Biblical warrior and heroine.

We are trying to get Josh's mom to stay with us and make sure the kids get the support they need. I am taking care of my psychological health by seeing both a psychiatrist and a social worker. We are doing the best we can, and it sounds as though the professionals think so too.

Again, the validation is important to me because I need to be a *right, good, responsible parent*. I need to do the right things so my kids will not suffer from the pain that I suffered. To this day I still carry around my battle wounds. I just want to live, DAMMIT!!!

Great news! The dean has approved Norma's leave of absence! I'm so happy and relieved, for until now I had been unable to see objectively that there really was a crisis. The fact that the process had turned out much easier than she anticipated shows it was the right decision. If it hadn't made sense that I needed her help, her colleagues would have resisted her leave-of-absence. And now I know for sure this is where she wants to be. Norma said, "They are my grandchildren. I want to be there for them and for you and Josh." I happily agreed.

Norma's postponement of her commitments to help us is a great gift from her heart and from God. I may have lost both my parents at a young age, but I feel blessed that this incredible woman has now come into my life. Her involvement in my life fills my ever-pressing yearning for that female role model.

Friday, December 5

This week has given me a small glimpse into the life of the elderly. I have difficulty going up and down stairs, I walk slowly, I can't drive myself, and my daily and weekly schedule is structured by a framework of appointments with doctors.

My stitches are finally out and the plastic surgeon said I can schedule my Biochemotherapy for the week of January 5th, which would give my foot plenty of time to heal. I went to the orthopedist, who wasn't happy to see I'd put too much weight on my foot. He did allow me to start physical therapy, but still forbade me from driving. Not being allowed to drive was driving me nuts.

My treatment was now scheduled for a month away. Even though I was eager and anxious to start the Biochemo as soon as possible, staying home for December is still really great. First, I can be around for Zach's fifth birthday party. Second, I can be home for Chanukah. I get to see Ozzie and Zach's expressions as they open the toys. We spoil them. Between all our family members they definitely get a gift each night, something neither Josh nor I had as kids.

CHAPTER 7 – Gearing Up for the Treatment

Getting Out of Bed and Other Emotional Hangovers

Josh

It's 8 AM.

Okay, so I broke. It's too much; I can't hold the weight. My strength is sapped- I am really exhausted. It's affecting Julie too. I can't control it—the emotion slips out.

I've trained for this moment my whole life- to be the strong, patient one—to absorb pain and guide it in positive directions. I've felt this way as a big brother, a father, a rabbi, teacher, manager, leader and now husband. Life is just not happening the way I imagined it would.

Thursday, December 11 – Sunday, December 14

Josh and I are away from the kids for a weekend focused on us, before we begin the period that will focus on me.

I had the best deep-tissue massage on Friday. This one kneaded every sore muscle in my body. I realize that since surgery—whether it's the trauma or the use of crutches—my body is stiff as a board. I scheduled another one for tomorrow after Shabbat.

Getting Out of Bed

As I leave the spa and walk with my cane to my villa — villa is the fancy way spas refer to apartments — I am constantly reminded that my body is not what it used to be.

I thought back to high school when a friend of mine suffered a spinal cord injury and became paralyzed from the waist down. This was a shock to the whole Jewish community because he was a beautiful and athletic young man. I remember reflecting that if it were me I would rather have died. During high school my life was basketball and I could not imagine life without my legs. This young man eventually made something positive from his situation and developed his own foundation for research into spinal cord injuries.

Now my priorities are different. I would like time to exercise, but my greatest concern is the wellbeing of my children. The surgery on my foot was traumatic but not as bad as I thought it would be. If I lost my whole foot it would have posed different challenges. Though I am slow, I surprise myself daily with the simple fact that I am learning to walk only on my big toe and the strange looking one next to it.

Now I am one of those people for whom others need to wait while I descend steps or walk down the street. It is humbling. There are so many little things I had taken for granted such as being able to run up and down the steps from our home to the car if I'd forgotten something. Now I have to be a lot more organized, and accepting of my pace and limitations.

Cancer is hard on people who care about the patient. My sister Caroline lives in Los Angeles and, because of the time difference, is rarely the first to hear news. My sister Deborah, who lives in Manhattan, has been so stressed about my situation that she menstruated three times in the past six weeks. She also blames me for her recent acne breakouts.

My medications, too, have been altered. My dosage of Prozac was raised. I take a prescribed sleeping pill because all my anxieties were manifesting at night. I would fall asleep from exhaustion and a few hours later would have a panic attack, which felt like a heart attack. So now I take Klonopin, 1 mg. three times a day, to ease the anxiety.

The person who has the hardest time going through this whole thing, apart from me, is Josh. The other day I found him not eating. I yelled at him, "Here I am trying to do everything to stay alive. I've chosen the most aggressive treatment—there can't be two sick adults in our household!"

It's Sunday morning, our last day at the spa. I was getting up for my meditation and yoga class. I peeked over at him and asked, "Are you getting up?"

He answered, "No. I'm not in the mood"

I responded in a firm voice, "You are getting up and I expect to see you at Meditation at 9 AM!"

It's hard for me to yell at him, but sometimes it seems he needs a kick in the behind to get up and face his day. I have those moments, too, when I feel lethargic and unmotivated, but I have enough experience with depression to know the signs, at least in others. When it continues for weeks, it is time to see a therapist.

Today I feel focused and strong and able to help him. I know there will be times when the roles will reverse and he'll have to force me out of bed. Last night Josh asked if I missed the kids. He said he missed the kids, which he definitely is *allowed* to do, but now I realize that last night he was already getting anxious. Of course I miss my children. But I also know I have to take care of myself. In the short term I may not be available to them, but I'm putting in this effort for the long haul. If that means staying at the Inn a little longer for one more meditation, yoga and massage, then it's worth it to me. This is the last fortification before my treatment on January 5. When I go home the countdown begins.

One of the strange things about cancer is that the patient usually looks fine, but it's the treatment that is so debilitating. I can't tell you how many people I bump into who are surprised to see me dressed and walking about. Someone might say, "Wow, Julie you look great!" The compliment is of course appreciated but then I ask myself, *what does she expect me to look like?*

Movement is one of my coping mechanisms. Even though my orthopedist had forbid me from walking and driving until January, I just can't obey. First, with the help of physical therapy, I am walking well on my foot. Second, driving is how I clear my mind and establish independence. The first month after surgery, I let my mother-in-law drive me everywhere. Others in the community volunteered to drive, and eventually stopped. The ball of my foot does not hurt—if anything it hurts more to walk around my house than to drive a car. When you have little children, walking with crutches or using a cane is cumbersome.

I spoke with two melanoma survivors who had received the same treatment as mine. One had been treated in Philadelphia and the other in Texas. They both said it's extremely debilitating. In addition to nausea and chills, both survivors lost more then twenty pounds with each round of Biochemo.

My whole life I've wanted to be five pounds lighter. Now I'm terrified I might lose weight and be too weak to speak with my children or begin the next round of treatment. I'm saying to myself, *I will eat even though eating makes me vomit, even if I develop mouth sores and even if I cannot stand up.*

The weeks before treatment must focus my mind, strengthen my body, and develop skills I'll need later.

Since diagnosis with the second melanoma, I've lost my appetite and also some weight. I bought a stop watch and set it to beep every two hours as a reminder to eat or drink. I want to enter treatment with a strong immune system. Having been warned about loss of appetite during treatment, I made a list for my mother-in-law of foods I like: cereal, peanut butter and jelly, pizza, ice cream, and chocolate. I know, it doesn't sound too healthy.

Monday, December 14

We got stuck in a snow storm, so we turned around and went back to the Inn. Even though Josh was anxious to see the kids, it was still nice to have one more night away. By morning all the roads were clear. During the drive home, I thought about Zach and how well he's adjusted to changes.

One day, when my foot wasn't bandaged and my stitches not yet removed, he walked into our room. I told him I was going to the hospital because my foot was sick, but didn't give details as to what the doctors would do. Zach was immediately drawn to my foot. I panicked because I hadn't rehearsed an explanation. Zach came onto the bed, close to my foot and then asked, "What are those black things on your foot?"

I answered, "Remember when you fell and got stitches on your chin? The doctors needed to put stitches on my foot." He sat a few moments quietly as if processing the information and said, "Okay, mom, I hope you feel better," and gave me a hug. I was in shock. He hadn't even noticed I was missing three toes!

Remembering how Zach reacted to my foot and his natural, uncomplicated understanding and acceptance, I think back to my childhood and wonder how much I knew about what was taking place at the time. I lived with a terminally ill mother and a depressed father. The time Josh spends with our children cannot begin to compare with my experiences as a child. I had practically no relationship with my father. When my mother died, my father's solution was to hire a nanny. We rarely talked about my mother. We rarely sat together as a family, except Friday nights which we kids called "Fight Nights."

My husband is nothing like my father. Josh is happy to spend time with our children. He asks if I'm jealous when the kids cry for him and not for me. I love it. Already my children live a different life than what I had as a child. I thank God for giving me the chance to bring up my children with love, self-confidence and security. I just beg to live—I've started to know what joy is about and I'm scared it could be snatched away.

Frustratingly, as soon as I began to feel better and recover from surgery Josh's attitude began to change. At first I was happy to see his feelings come out. It was only normal for him to react to what we were going through, but the questions he voiced started to destabilize my own confidence.

What is the purpose of life?
Where is God; why is this happening to us?
Is there real happiness in the world?

I too have questioned the purpose of life. I felt angry when there was no Mother's Day in my house. At age 21, with my father's illness and death, the question resurfaced: *what is the point of living when all I experience is pain and suffering?* Eventually I realized that if I focused on unanswerable questions I would never become a survivor.

I had neither patience nor answers for Josh's questions. Just listening to Josh voice his anger was undermining my faith in God. The quality of our life as a couple was beginning to deteriorate.

We developed a signal for communicating our feelings to each other. The key sentence was, "*I need to share a feeling.*" That's the cue to get the other to start listening.

I told him his questions were affecting my spirits. He listened but then explained that, although our weekend away had been good for me it had not been good for him. He'd tried to be a good sport by joining the meditations, yoga, and massage but, overall, the excess time spent alone with his thoughts was making him depressed.

I understood we were coping in different ways. For me, the weekend had been the ultimate escape. I said to Josh, "If I question the meaning of life and why this is happening to me, what is going to keep me from giving up? I need to keep my faith in God solid. It's keeping me alive and I don't want to die. I want to be here and I want us to get through it together." In realizing the pressure and stress, we both began to cry.

We are driving back to New York and I say to Josh that I love him. He'd said it the day before, though he knows my feeling, it would help to hear it more often. Interestingly, to say, "I love you," makes me aware of my love for him.

Until now we had been wary of sharing our fears. How could it help Josh if I'd constantly told him my fear of dying, when he was trying to deal with the fear of becoming a single father with three small children?

Tuesday, December 16

I woke up at 6 AM. For the past few weeks my Palm Pilot has been dead and I never Hot-Synced it. Now, when I could benefit from an organizer to schedule doctors' appointments and new phone numbers, I have nothing to use. I have many phone numbers I need to organize: personal numbers, my doctors', my childrens', their therapists', my therapists', my friends', my family, work and personal numbers I should always have on me like my like our health insurance and Social

Security numbers. My Palm Zire arrived last night, but I only had energy to work on it this morning.

This morning I got into a 'zone' whereby I was going to activate the Palm, read the instructions and learn how to use the Hot-Sync. So there I was, fixated on how to get the Palm to work, while my mother-in-law and babysitter attended to getting my children ready for school.

Later, reflecting on the morning with my mother-in-law, I said, "Thank you for helping my kids get dressed and off to school today." I don't always thank her because there have been mornings when I clearly couldn't help out. Now that I was recovering, I felt there was not much of an excuse so I said, "I was a little distracted. I didn't mean to take advantage of your being here."

I had given her an opportunity to discuss something that had been on her mind for a while. The truth is that I have always encouraged her to be honest with me; but now that she was being honest I couldn't handle it. Norma's response was, "Yes I see that you are distracted, but what I am also seeing is you are distracting yourself from your children — last night at bedtime and this morning while they were getting ready for school."

I said, "I was aware of what was going on but I felt between you, Josh, and the babysitter you had everything under control. I didn't hear any screaming and then I just got into a zone working on the computer."

She answered, "Yes I know that Josh and I were there, but I want to let you know that when you distance yourself from your children, I see them distancing themselves from you. I know this is something you are sensitive about because you felt your mother separated herself from you as she was dying. I am sure you do not intend to give your children that feeling."

I felt angry and wanted to say, "It's not your job to tell me what my mother did and what I should avoid!" Instead, I tried to put aside my defensiveness and answered calmly, "It's normal right now to be distracted and there will be times I'll need to escape and I won't be available to them. That's why we asked you to be here and, God willing, when this is all over I will have the chance to make up for lost time."

I feel very close to my mother-in-law and want her esteem and good opinion of me. Her words have the ability to imprint on my brain and tear me apart because I love her so much. I value her judgment and feel guilty to disappoint her.

I ended up talking about this with my psychiatrist, who acknowledged my momentary need for distractions. Josh and my mother-in-law both see my detachment as part of a larger piece. That I am trying to protect them in the event of my death, as my mother had for me.

I have memories of me screaming for my mother. The babysitter is literally holding me back and dragging me into my room for bedtime. I remember looking for a reaction on my mother's face that perhaps my histrionics would get some attention. She didn't even turn her head or flinch. She just continued to watch the television, as if nothing was happening.

I work hard at correcting the things I felt harmed me as a child, which makes me an easy target for guilt. I know I have given my children attention, time, and energy. The next few months are going to be tough—I need some slack. We're all anxious and don't know what to expect.

My psychiatrist suggested that, if my mother-in-law or Josh feel I'm being detached, she or he can say, "go ask mommy to read you a book," or "give mommy a kiss before you leave for your bus." I thought that technique would help pull me out of the fog in which I seemed to be frequently enveloped.

I finally got the phone numbers into my Palm Zire for my mother-in-law, to organize the household in case I'll be out of commission. She will have to manage my three children's crazy school and after-school schedules. I was overwhelmed just thinking about it.

CHAPTER 8

Birthdays

Josh

I just wasted $19.95 plus tax. No. I know the kids really appreciate the thought, and gift giving is part of any father child relationship. But I'm starting to get a little resentful about all these toys and games I keep buying them. It's not that the car, doll, game, DVD or whatever-they-saw-in-the-store-that-they-just-had-to-have-or-they-won't-stop-screaming will be played with only two or three times before it becomes one amongst hundreds of toys that join the ever-increasing pile for neglected items. That's fine.

It's not even the waste. Julie is very good at making sure toys that aren't played with after a few weeks get brought to the right shelter, charity, or Salvation Army-drop off. It's also not that sometimes we shed a toy too soon only to have to run out again and buy the same one before they notice that it's missing.

The point is that it's none of these things that I resent. It's that their favorite toy, the one that never gets boring, can always be poked, stepped on, jumped off of, kicked, pulled, pushed, the toy that needs no batteries—unless you include beer and food, though not necessarily in that order—is good ole dad. Who needs jungle gyms when you can have dad? Who needs superhero toys, when you can have dad?

I'm not sure when I became a Super Dad, but I know I wasn't always him. Growing up I learned to appreciate the importance of an involved father. Not that my dad didn't chip in. But as "liberated" and "feminist" an age we lived in, my mother did most of the stuff around the house and with us children.

So, it was easy for me to envision a marriage relationship where the household responsibilities belonged to Julie, and I could play a role on the educational, role modeling and emotional planes. But it was not to be.

With all the wonderful things Julie brought to the table, one that was lacking was management: from house cleaning to budgeting to losing her keys, she always seemed too scattered to make order in our lives. Later we would uncover this as symptomatic of adult attention-deficit/hyperactivity disorder (AD/HD), which still didn't help me get the place clean or balance the budget.

All of this hit like a ton of bricks when Zach arrived. I simply did not have the energy to take care of my full time job, full time school, marriage and kids. I knew that the schooling would end soon, and luckily realized I had chosen the wrong career path, but as I struggled to the finish line on both my frustration grew not with Zach, nor with fatherhood, but Julie. These problems never really went away, and in fact were exacerbated by the mounting health issues that greeted us at every turn.

The months—now years—of surgeries and treatments, back-and-forth to hospitals in other states, waking at 5 o'clock and going all day, taking on the routines, the emotional foundation for the family, while trying to pay the bills, balance the budget, manage the house and be the best husband and father I can be, have left me bruised, scarred, and emotionally exhausted.

However, the other day Julie was doing carpool for Zach and his friends, when she asked them what they wanted to be when they grew up: Policeman—Superhero—Doctor—Harry Potter. Zach answered that he wanted to be a daddy. I could live a thousand lives, see all there is to see, and still nothing might compare to that.

Wednesday, December 17

Zach's birthday! I cannot believe he is five years old. Josh, Norma, and I bring a cake to his class party.

When Josh, Norma, and I entered the classroom, Zach jumped out of his seat and yelled, "Daddy, daddy! Can I give you a hug? Everyone, this is my daddy!" I'm usually happy for Josh that he and Zach have such a close relationship, but at times like this I feel insecure—especially when my mother-in-law's voice still rings in my head, that my children are distancing themselves from me. So I say to myself, "What am I? Chopped liver! I'm the one who baked and decorated your Thomas the Tank Engine cake! I got you presents for all your friends; I was the one who told daddy to come!"

I kept my feelings contained and Zach helped me pass out the plates to his friends. He loved blowing out the candles. We were all so proud when, after eating, he threw out his plate without being asked. Zach handed a Chinese yo-yo to each of his friends and teachers. There was one left. I asked him in front of his class to whom he should give the last yo-yo. I was trying to suggest that perhaps he would want to bring it home for Ozzie who was having a hard time with all the presents Zach was getting. Then Zach surprised me, and he said "Mommy, I want you to have the last yo-yo." My heart melted. Despite my insecurity, he still loved me.

Later in the day I got a haircut. I've been anxious about losing hair. I'm not supposed to lose all of it, but am supposed to expect thinning. When I went to the Cancer Center in Philadelphia a woman told me she'd shaved her head to avoid being freaked out by chunks of hair falling out. If my hair were long enough, I would shave it and donate it to someone who needed a wig. But it's not. So I went to the hairdresser with the idea that my hair be cut to chin length. The hairdresser had a better idea, having had experience with clients undergoing chemotherapy. He suggested, "If you don't want short hair there is no point in cutting it short. Rather, it would be helpful to add more layers to your hair. The layers make your hair lighter—it's the weight of the hair that makes it fall out." He convinced me and I liked my haircut.

When Josh noticed my drastic haircut he made fun of me and said I had too much time on my hands. His suggestion was, "Why don't you just deal with it when the time comes?" His point may have been logical but I had an emotional need for this haircut. I need to feel I am being proactive because it eases my anxiety. Just to wait for something that might happen would cause me terrible angst. Hair loss or not, it's still a nice haircut and it makes me feel good.

Thursday, December 18

My babysitter couldn't show up for work today, but Norma quickly stepped up to the task and got my kids dressed, packed their lunch boxes and put them on their buses.

Once again this was a morning when I got distracted. While Norma was putting Ozzie on the bus, Marsha was whining beside my leg and wanting me to pick her up. At that moment, I felt she could be ignored. Josh entered the room and picked her up. I asked him, "Why did you pick her up?"

Josh said, "Because she was crying."

I answered, "She wasn't really crying, she was whining."

Josh responds, "You know, you could really stop what you are doing and get on the floor and play with her."

I didn't know where all this was coming from but I picked up Marsha and held her until Norma was ready to take her outside for a walk.

Ten minutes later Josh called from work and said, "I feel like you're mad at me."

I said, "I feel like you're mad at me!"

He said, "All I did was pick up Marsha to say good-bye and you snapped at me asking why I was picking her up."

I told him I was feeling sensitive and that his picking her up implied a criticism of me. Once again I said, "I'm allowed to be distracted. She was whining because she had to wait for her turn to go outside."

Josh said, "I wasn't blaming you."

I said, "Okay, good-bye."

Minutes later I call him back at work and say, "I just wanted to say that I love you."

Josh asks, "Is everything okay?"

"Yes, I just wanted to tell you that I love you."

"Are you sure everything is okay?"

"Yes!"

Later I met with my psychiatrist and the issue that Norma brought to my attention was rehashed — the topic of me distancing myself from my children. He said he had a different view of the situation: "You could be a little more sympathetic and realize that living in your house, taking care of you and Josh, is no easy task. This is a huge sacrifice on her part. It doesn't take away from the fact that she still wants to help you, but perhaps she was simply annoyed."

I later relayed the conversation to Josh to ask what he thought of my psychiatrist's assessment of his mother. Josh said, "It is possible that my mother was annoyed, but you also know the hours between 7 AM to 8 AM and 5 AM to 7 PM are the most difficult hours of the day. If you are going to be distracted then just get out of the way. It doesn't help for you to be sitting in a place nearby while we are all trying to get the kids out to school and you are spaced out on the computer."

This conversation between Josh and me is ironic. I used to nudge him to be attentive to the kids and now I am the one who is out to lunch. He used to come home and, before saying hello to the kids, would look at the mail or listen to messages on the machine. He would get mad at me as if I was dumping the kids as soon as he got home, when the truth was they were so excited to see him they would jump on him. I am very proud of Josh — his comments on being attentive reflect his growth and skill as a parent.

Yet, I feel guilty that I'm not living up to my own expectations. It's funny how things come full circle. I used to think, "Why is Josh so inattentive — doesn't he realize I could use his help when all three kids are screaming at the same time? I realize he had his own distractions and was feeling overwhelmed.

Josh's latest realization is that life is not about happiness. He was brought up expecting happiness and now he is inundated with stress and despair. I explain to myself that life contains both but we can work through troubles, gain understanding and find some joy in each moment.

An example: I said to Zach, "Do you know how much I love you?"

He responded, with a shrug of the shoulders, "No."

I said, as we were standing in the kitchen, "I love you from this side of the kitchen all the way over to the other side."

He started giggling and then for the first time he reciprocated and asked me, "Do you know how much I love you?"

I said, "No."

He hesitated for a moment because he was thinking and then he said, "I love you from the floor to the ceiling." I was shocked and elated. My heart swelled with joy. I gave him a big hug and kiss and told him how special he is.

Saturday night, December 20

In preparation for the first night of Chanukah, I went to Circuit City and bought Josh a DVD and Dual Video Combo. I thought it was pretty cool and told him about it. The next thing I knew we were returning it. I guess I had entered a sacred place of electronics where men like to make their own decisions.

Then I had another idea. We take many pictures but hide them away in albums. I was never much of a picture person. I didn't want to remember anything about growing up.

In trying to overcome that inclination, I felt it was time to put pictures of our family in Josh's office and around our house. We have been living in this house almost four years and I haven't hung one picture on the wall. One of our common excuses was that neither Josh nor I knew how to use a power drill.

I was determined. I went to Home Depot, bought a power drill and got a guy at the store to show me how to use it. By the time Josh came home to light both Chanukah and Shabbat candles, we had pictures around our living room and on the wall, two lithographs, and the beautiful *Megillah* (Book of Esther, written on parchment, read on the holiday of Purim) and its beautiful wooden case that Josh inherited from his grandfather. I was so proud of myself. In addition, I also bought a bookcase to display our albums in the living room—the kids haven't stopped asking to look at the pictures.

When Josh came home he smiled, but I wanted him to know how much effort went into this project—not to make him feel guilty but to let him know that it was a gift from the heart. I think there was something else I wanted to tell Josh through my efforts: *I'm finally moving in and this is my home.* Before this I had never invested myself personally into the house because there always was a chance we might move somewhere else but now I was letting him know that I was home and I am going to *live* in this home.

CHAPTER 9
"Go Doctor, Go! You Can Do it!"

Monday, December 22

I am presently trying to calm down from three hours of hell. I have already taken Tylenol, am listening to a meditation tape and have just opened a beer. Nothing happened today that has never happened before; it was just one of those days.

Today was Zach and Ozzie's monthly visit to the allergist. It usually takes forty-five minutes to an hour to get there because he is not the typical allergist and his office is some distance away. If I wanted a typical allergist I could find one a few blocks away. These visits are always challenging because I take the boys as soon as they get off the bus. I know to prepare snacks and drinks.

There I am waiting outside with both car doors open to claim my children from the bus—if they enter the house they go directly to the television. Ozzie gets home first so I put him in the car. A few minutes later Zach comes off the bus and he's already crying. He's upset that he's missing the Chanukah party at his after-school Hebrew program. When I had scheduled the appointment there was no way to know it would conflict with his Chanukah schedule. I try validating Zach's feelings, and then remind him that he just had a huge gymnastics party which happened to also be on Chanukah but, of course, he wasn't thinking along that line.

Now we're in the car and on our way. The first whine comes from Zach, "I'm hungry! What do you have?" I give him a few choices but he does not like any of my offerings. He eventually accepts defeat and eats the brownies I brought for him. Then he whines, "I'm thirsty!"

Trying to remain calm, I say, "What would you like to drink."

He says, "Juice."

I pass him back a juice box while I keep my eyes on the road.

Then the next whiner chimes in, "I want brownies and juice." Ozzie is almost three and has to have everything Zach has. I know in advance to prepare double of everything. Zach finishes his juice box in one slurp and immediately asks for another. From past experience, pulling over on the highway and having Zach pee in a cup or a bottle, I tell him he has to wait and could have another juice on the way home from the doctor.

The next argument is about which DVD they should watch and they cannot reach an agreement. When we bought the car with the DVD player we had in mind the long driving trips we make to Montreal to see Josh's parents. Initially I stuck by the rule that DVD watching was only for long trips. Soon the rule was reduced to any car ride longer than five minutes. I just can't stand the screaming and whining. In my head I am screaming and yelling at them while Zach pushes his feet into the back of my chair. Even though I want to yell, I don't. This may explain the onset of a migraine that I am presently feeling.

Eventually we arrive at the doctor's office. Zach is a very experienced patient and is not afraid of needles. Ozzie, on the other hand, only has to be told that he is going to the doctor and he begins to whimper. Before we even get to the shots, the doctor has to review with me the progress of both boys over the past month. I am calmly trying to explain Ozzie's progress while he is screaming in the background and Zach, oblivious to everything, is going round and round in circles in the corner. Zach likes to walk in circles with an occasional humming. This drives me *nuts*.

I manage to finish giving the doctor each child's monthly report and Zach easily jumps up on the table to receive his shot. He's truly amazing. When I take him to the local blood clinic all the elderly patients in the waiting room are so impressed with him that he doesn't scream or put up a fight. Zach says to the doctor, "Just give it to me already!"

Zach is done, but now the hard part begins; it's Ozzie's turn. He begins screaming as I try to hold him in place. The doctor places a rubber band around his arm because he receives his medication intravenously, but the doctor pricks him and he can't find the vein. The doctor then tries the other arm as Ozzie's screams get louder and again he can't find the vein. A third time; the doctor tries an area around Ozzie's wrist and he still can't find the vein. Ozzie at this point is in hysterics and there is Zach in the background cheering the doctor on, "Go doctor, go! You can do it!" I tell Zach to be quiet. After three failed attempts of trying to get into Ozzie's vein the doctor gives up.

This is followed by the ride home, but it happens to be a day that Zach also has Karate class. I have his outfit in the car with us but now we have to try to make it in time. Meanwhile, Ozzie is crying that his arm hurts and that he is tired and then Zach chimes in, "I'm tired, too, and I don't want to go to Karate."

Zach does not get to make those decisions but to avoid confrontation I tell him, "Okay, we'll be home soon." As we get closer to Karate I call Josh to meet us there so I can just drop off Zach without having to park and take both boys out of the car.

Zach overhears my conversation with Josh and says, "Where are we going? I thought we were going home." I tell him that we are going to Karate and he immediately begins to whine, "I'm too tired for Karate."

So I respond, "Okay, so Ozzie will have your lesson instead."

Then Ozzie's radar picks up and he says, "Wadi, Ozzie go to Wadi?" Ozzie is too young for Karate and is always upset when Zach goes without him.

Anyway, Zach immediately says," Fine," when the thought occurs to him that Ozzie might replace him.

Josh meets us at the Karate place as I pull up and let Zach out of the car. Ozzie sees Josh and the Karate place and begins to cry, "Daddy, Karate, daddy, Karate...." I try to calm him down and tell him that daddy will be home soon.

I finally pull into my driveway and now Ozzie whines that he wants me to carry him out of the car and up the steps. Mind you, I have been driving against doctor's orders and I definitely should not be carrying a 32-pound child. But I can't take the whining and the crying anymore and despite my pain, I just pick him up and bring him inside.

Once I'm inside I run to the bathroom because I had been holding it in all day. I think I finally get five minutes to myself when I hear Ozzie crying, "Mommy, mommy, I want television." After relieving myself, I tell him that he has to eat dinner before television and, thank God, he actually listens to that one. Josh finally gets home with Zach and the whining stops for about five minutes in order to light the Chanukah candles.

Then Zach asks, "Where is my spaceship present?"

I answer, "What makes you think you're getting a spaceship present."

Zach answers quite frankly, "It's been in your closet for the past few days."

I hold in my immediate frustration and tell Zach, "There are still four more nights of Chanukah and tonight is not the night for spaceships. And stop looking in my closet!"

I finally sit down and say to Josh, "Tag, you're it." I tell him for the past three hours the kids have been saying "Mommy" at the beginning and end of each sentence: "Mommy, I want juice, mommy. Mommy, I'm tired, mommy." I tell Josh that if I hear my name called one more time I'm going to lose my mind.

Thank God Josh immediately takes over and I have the opportunity to write this out, and decompress as I drink my beer. The crazy thing is that this was a normal day. It had nothing to do with my cancer or Biochemotherapy. I would have felt crazy even without this stuff in the back of my mind. But since I do have all these things in my head and I'm trying to keep life as normal as possible for my kids, I thought that tonight I was going to lose it.

I have finally calmed down and it is time to put the kids to bed. It becomes funny when you start counting down the hours, minutes, and seconds until bedtime and then all of a sudden a little tug comes to your heart when you see how cute they are in their pajamas and snuggled into bed. I love my kids so much even if it pains me when they do their jobs so well in pressing all of my buttons and driving me crazy.

I must go soon because Ozzie is calling for me. He's saying, "Mommy, lie down in my bed?" How can I deprive him or myself of that opportunity to cuddle with him especially after the day we have just had and my guilt at having to leave him soon when I begin treatment? What if something should happen to me? I love lying in his bed and listening as his breathing becomes gradually slower and slower as he enters a deeper and deeper sleep.

Tuesday, December 23

I went back to the orthopedist for a follow-up visit before going to Philadelphia for the Biochemo. Despite his orders over the past two weeks I bought myself orthopedic shoes with commercial orthotics. In being taught how to walk with a cane it was helpful to have supportive shoes. So, even though I preempted my doctor's suggestion, he complimented me on a choice of shoes that provided ankle support. I then said, "I have a question for you and I want you to say yes!"

He said, "Yes, but it depends."

I asked him, "Can I drive?"

"Have you driven already?"

I blushed. "I drove myself into the city." Before I gave him a chance to pass judgment I said, "It's easier to drive than it is to walk around my house!"

He gave me a look that said, "You should have waited until you had my permission, but you're doing well." I felt I could be myself with him. He told me my foot had only a little more healing to do, and to come back in six weeks for a customized orthotic fitting to be scheduled.

At present I'm walking slowly and have to work on my balance.

The customized orthotic will help me with the balance problem. I'm excited because I think I'll be able to run again. I'm already almost running up and down the stairs in my house just trying to take care of my kids. I'm optimistic about my foot. The operation came out much better than I imagined.

Wednesday, December 24

I woke up this morning with a terrible headache. I tried using one of my meditation tapes to breathe out the headache—that didn't work. Then I tried a twenty five minute yoga session—that did work.

Thursday, December 25

Zach's school is on break so for the next two weeks we are sending him to Yeshiva Ketana, where he will go next year. Ozzie had his first play-date this morning and then two high school girls came to volunteer a few hours as my babysitter had the day off. This community is amazing with volunteers. They refused the money I offered.

Josh and I took the day to see a movie. Unfortunately we chose a very long one, *Lord of the Rings*, the final film in the trilogy. We had seen the previous two and liked this one but it was *four* hours long. I could hardly sit still by the end. There were just too many thoughts racing in my head. When Josh and I returned from the movie, Zach was already home and we had three kids jumping up and down excited to see us. I felt overwhelmed; four hours until bedtime. I spent time on the computer and then cleaned the kitchen. I realized I was purposely distracting myself from being with the children. I felt a stress headache or a migraine coming on. So instead of remaining in this "distracted" state that no one seems to appreciate, I was able to step outside myself and realize that I needed a "time-out." I told Josh I was having a hard time coping and needed some time alone. Josh told me he appreciated that.

As I go through the calendar and mark the days I had seen doctors, between October and December, I get an anxiety attack and realize why I had so little patience for my children. Just seeing the list of appointments for that period has a tremendous effect on me. Many events from the time I had surgery appear to be blocked from memory. At times the hospital had me so drugged up that I barely remember the people who visited. Now that I'm trying to piece everything together I get post-traumatic stress from all that has happened, which surprises me because I thought I was handling things so well. Now, as I recognize and deal with the anxiety, I lock myself in the bathroom and listen to a meditation tape before seeing my children.

Then I completely lost my patience, which I can't say was unexpected. I finished giving the children dinner and then put them all in the bath. I thought I could leave the bathroom briefly to make a quick phone call to a friend and cancel dinner plans as I was too stressed to think of trying to relax and have dinner out.

While I am on the phone I hear Zach and Ozzie arguing in the bathroom. I hang up the phone quickly and run back to the bathroom. I see Zach's arm tightly clenching Ozzie's neck.

Now most likely Ozzie instigated this episode by taking away one of Zach's toys and Zach was just trying to get it back. I walked into the bathroom and yelled, "I do not like what you boys are doing!" I took the toy out of Ozzie's hand that Zach was trying to retrieve. Zach already began to cry because the tone of my voice was so severe. I said to him, "Do you remember what happened the last time you were playing silly in the bath? You slipped and I had to take you to the doctor to put stitches under your chin. This is not the way to play in the bath." Zach continued to cry while Ozzie and Marsha sat there silently. I think they were in a state of shock. I asked Zach, "Why are you crying?"

He said, "I don't like it when you speak in that voice." I responded, "I am sorry if the way that I spoke scared you but I only used that voice because what you and Ozzie were doing was very dangerous and that scared me." Zach continued to pout and whimper but when I said, "Zach, it's over. I'm not mad at you; I just want you to play more safely in the bath," he immediately calmed down and left the bathroom to watch television.

On the other hand, I am not fine. I feel as though I totally lost control. I hate yelling and although I know my yelling was in context of trying to prevent my children from being injured, I hate this anxious feeling that comes along with it. I already feel guilty that I yelled because if I had not been in a bad mood at the outset maybe I would have handled the situation differently.

The bottom line is everyone is fine. Bedtime is twenty-five minutes away and counting and then I will kiss them good night and tell them I love them. I'm just wiped out physically — and, especially, emotionally.

The kids are finally asleep and I say to Josh, "I'm feeling insecure because I raised my voice at Zach. Are you mad at me?"

He said, "No. Just today I had to raise my voice at Ozzie because he kept head-butting me and it really hurt. I told him, Stop! He started to cry, but he didn't do it again." Then, Josh said to me in a comforting way, "Julie, it is okay if we change our tone of voice to alert our kids about something serious."

I walked away for a minute and realized I have maintained a positive outlook even though Biochemotherapy is less than two weeks away. The situation we are all dealing with is hard, and then I'm hard on myself for being in a bad mood. The truth is I am probably entitled to have many more bad moods and ones that last even longer than today's. I just don't like feeling angry. I need to give myself a break. I'm trying to forgive myself for being imperfect.

Friday, December 26

I had physical therapy first thing in the morning and then came home for my scheduled massage. Until recently I thought massages were a luxury or at least a special treat. However, since my diagnosis I have allowed myself to receive weekly massages and have come to realize they are therapeutic.

The massage is going great but then I hear Marsha crying through the door. I decide to have her seen by a doctor because tonight is Shabbat and if anything erupts over the weekend I will have to wait until Sunday to see the doctor.

I take a deep breath. I feel like there is a lot going on. It's now 1:09 PM. and her appointment is for 2:45 PM. I'm going to try to take a nap for an hour — while the boys will, I hope, stay downstairs.

My alarm rings to wake me in time for the doctor's appointment, but I desperately need more sleep. I get up, get dressed and take Marsha to the doctor. It's Friday afternoon and Shabbat is starting at 4:16 PM. We get to the doctor's office and it is 3:30 PM. and we have yet to be seen. We're finally seen and the doctor checks out Marsha.

The doctor then asks me, "How's your foot?" At the moment I am in a good mood and I say, "Great," as I show him that I can now jump up and down. He asked me when my treatment is due to start. For some reason, I answer in a perky voice, "January 5." We leave the doctor's office and I feel fine but I need to get something done before Shabbat. I call Josh on my way home so he can be ready to receive Marsha while I run back out fifteen minutes before Shabbat to buy a gift for our hosts the following day. Josh tells me he is losing his mind because the boys are jumping all over him but he will still be ready to get Marsha.

I know it's crazy but I don't want to show up at these people's house empty-handed. I get to the wine store, buy a few bottles, make it to our friend's house in time before Shabbat and drop off the wine. The next thing on my drive home I start crying. I keep fooling myself that everything is okay but then I see the doctor and then I see my friend, who both ask me briefly how I'm doing and when my treatment is starting. Driving in the car, reality hits me — *everything is not okay.* I'm scared of the upcoming treatment. I don't know what to do to prepare for the treatment and there is nothing I can do anyway. I've been reading about macrobiotic diets and their success with cancer prevention but my oncologist is not a supporter of that path. I'm dying from sitting and waiting for this treatment to begin. I have terrible anxiety and need to keep myself occupied. Although it helps to write as an outlet, I remain frustrated.

Saturday night, December 27

I can't sleep! Last night Marsha was crying. I was finally in a deep sleep and I so badly wanted her to put herself back to sleep. I eventually got up and picked her up, realizing she had diarrhea. I changed her diaper and she didn't want to go back to bed. Then I warmed up some almond milk for her — she is gluten and casein free. I rocked her a little, then I put her in the crib and she fell back to sleep.

Five minutes later Marsha starts screaming. This time it is Josh's turn. I say to him, "She must be teething. Give her some Tylenol." Josh can't find the Tylenol and then I start helping him look and I can't find the Motrin either. I begin to panic. How can we have no Tylenol or Motrin in the house? These are basic requirements in any household with children! It then occurs to me that maybe her stomach is bothering her because she does have diarrhea. I find the Imodium in the dark and pour a little into a medicine cup having no idea what the proper dosage is. Josh gives it to her and she soon calms down. Minutes later, she falls asleep on his shoulder.

But now I can't sleep! I can normally fall asleep easily from exhaustion but am up a few hours later and cannot get back to sleep. What do I do? I had already taken my sleeping pill for the night. I decide to take melatonin. I take one and am then up again in a few hours and it's still dark outside. It's now about 6 o'clock in the morning and I'm upstairs writing on the couch in the living room. I'm hiding because I don't want my boys (who are already downstairs playing nicely) to find me. I need a few more minutes of calm before the chaos begins. I hear them coming up the steps. I sink into the couch to hide, trying to be as quiet as possible. Then they run back downstairs. Phew! Oh, no, Zach is up the stairs again and Ozzie is following him. I don't know how they can be so busy so early in the morning. Now I'm just worried Marsha's going to wake up and then I'll really have to appear because she can't play by herself. I remain sunken into the couch, working on my rhythmic breathing, hoping not to be found for just a few more minutes. I know it's going to be a long day. I need to pace myself. I don't like it when I'm wound up and feeling on the verge of losing my patience.

I am hard on myself about losing patience. My father lacked patience and he would just yell as an opportunity to let off steam from the day, but in the process I would feel ridiculed and humiliated.

Oh, no! I've been found. My boys run to me at the couch and say, "Mommy, mommy, we didn't see you." I answer, "I was just sitting here quietly." Zach asks, "Can I sit here quietly with you?" Then Ozzie brings his "Blankie" and we are all nestled on the couch. Despite my anxiety about being found, I am happy to see them.

I don't want my children to pay for my past or present traumas. Everyone tells me my expectations are unrealistic and that my children are natural extensions of me. But, hey, I am not a natural extension of my father. I've worked very hard to be where I am today as a parent. So I try hard and even harder with my children. I take comfort that whatever they are feeling concerning my operation and upcoming Biochemotherapy; they will *never* experience the traumas that I experienced as a child. I am their mom and want to protect them from harm. I am scared for them and myself. I pray that we will all get through this with negligible scars. I still have happy moments as I anticipate my treatment; it's just the unknown that's eating away at me. I'm frustrated that I don't know what to expect, that I cannot control the situation.

How sick will I be? My friends want to visit me in Philadelphia. I don't know if I should encourage them to make the more than two hours' drive when I don't know if I will be awake or sleeping. When I get home will I be able to see them? Will I be able to give them some or any attention? How will Josh deal with all this? The three months will be difficult. It is hard to see these months through. You crave for it all to be over and then you have to go back for another month of treatment. I hope Josh and my children will be able to forgive me when I can't give them the attention they all need. I also hope, when this is all finished, I can make up for lost time.

And then the guilt sets in. My whole childhood was bounded by rules to play quietly; not to disturb my sick mother, and now my children will have to be given the same instructions. I remember that sadness and loneliness I felt as a child because I didn't have an attentive babysitter or close playmates.

I try to convince myself it will be different. My mother had been given a terminal diagnosis. Presently, I am cancer-free. Unfortunately, I have a 60-percent chance of reoccurrence if I don't do anything. That is why I am choosing a preventative treatment—because I don't want my diagnosis to be terminal.

In the meantime, I thank God that my mother-in-law will be around to give my children the love, attention and nurturing they need. I don't feel she is replacing me. I am grateful my children have the familial support I lacked. I had an ill mother who later died, a distant father, a hired governess, and family members I was not allowed to see because, as my father would say, *they are all crazy!* His words poisoned our view of the people who could have helped us when we needed it.

My children, on the other hand, have incredibly nurturing paternal grandparents. I have two sisters and a brother. Josh has two brothers and a sister. All eagerly wait for my request for help. My mother's three sisters constantly call and offer to keep me company in the hospital. It must pain them that the child of their dead sister is sick with cancer and also has young children, like the situation my mom was in when she became sick. I assume it brings back bad memories for them as well.

I know it was hard for my mother's family when my sister Deborah named her daughter Marsha. It was difficult initially for everyone to say the name. My grandmother was one of the first to say, "I better start calling her Marsha now or I will never be able to do it." My grandmother is not always coherent these days but she understood this well. So when, two years later, my Marsha arrived I think everyone felt more comfortable. I hope the name comforted them as well as it comforted me.

If my father were alive, I'm unsure how helpful he would be. If my mother were alive, I wouldn't know what to expect from her because I hardly remember her. I just wish I had a mommy, especially now.

Sunday, December 28

Today was the last day of Chanukah. About ten days ago when I was still wavering over which treatment I should commit to — Biochemotherapy or a different treatment in a New York hospital, much less aggressive but equally experimental — my oncologist in Philadelphia recommended putting off the decision and enjoying the eight days of Chanukah, one of my favorite holidays.

It is one of the few lasting memories I have of my mother. After we would make the blessings and light the candles, we all sat down and sang *Ma Oz Tzur*. I still hear her voice in my head. My mother had a Conservative background and didn't pronounce all the Hebrew words properly. I used to giggle when I heard her sing but still remember it.

From then on, Chanukah went downhill. One year my father made an effort to buy us chocolate Chanukah gelt (chocolate coins). It was so disappointing that I decided to give my requests in advance. Then one year he made the announcement, "Why should I give Chanukah presents, when I give presents all year round!"

I remember one Chanukah when I saved up enough money to buy my stepmother a Ralph Lauren robe. I couldn't find her size, but thought I would bring it home anyway and she could return it for something she liked. I was proud of myself because the previous summer I had my first paid job as a counselor where I earned $350. The robe cost $200 and I was so proud of myself because I had earned the money myself.

I wanted to show I was responsible because in sixth grade I had come to be known as the family thief. When something was missing I would be called in. During my stepmother's second year in New York she didn't understand why I had to bring a present for a bat mitzvah party. I was embarrassed to attend without a gift and stole $40 from my stepmother's wallet.

Now I was in tenth grade and earned my own money. I wanted to show her my level of growth and responsibility. I was so proud of myself in giving her the robe. She smiled and said thank you. The next day I returned home from school to see a check for two hundred dollars on my desk. It was made out to me over her signature. I was bewildered. What could this be? When I went to ask her she said, "The robe wasn't in my size anyway, and I won't take money from you."

I was so disappointed that I said, "We could have returned it together and picked out something else that you liked." She said, "Thank you, but no thank you," and walked away. I was so hurt that I ran to my room and cried. I was sixteen years old and had reached out to the only mother figure I had. I felt rejected. Why couldn't she say that while the $200 meant nothing to her, it was a fortune and considerable sacrifice for me?

I never bought her another present.

I never had many new toys. As an adult, I can spend hours in a toy store. Our children do receive gifts every night of Chanukah, but they are not all from Josh and me. Each night we give the kids gifts from different family members. The children are definitely spoiled but I am just as excited as they are when they open their presents.

I made an effort to go to the synagogue today. I was finally able to walk. I think being sick makes people feel uncomfortable. That is why I made an effort to get dressed nicely like when, before beginning treatment, I said good-bye to my students. I wanted them to see that I still look the same.

Tomorrow is Sunday, which leaves me one week to get organized. I have to make sure of all the phone numbers for my mother-in-law, the list of after-school activities, carpools, doctor's appointments, and medications. I'm sure it will all go fine, but I can't help feeling that I'm abandoning my children. I feel abandoned by my mother.

After my first melanoma surgery nine days after Marsha's birth, I had the choice to stay overnight at the hospital but because I had just spent five days with Marsha in the hospital, recovering from a Cesarean section, I felt my children needed my presence for their sense of stability, even if I'm only resting in my room. They want their mommy. I reflect on the possibility that my children might not be secure about mommy or daddy's always being there. Nowadays when I hear Zach gloat to someone, "My mommy made me this or that." I smile to myself because I realize I have been there for him and he can rely on me to care for him.

That is my job. I am here to care for them, feed them, and nurture them. Who ever lost sleep over me, a live-in nanny?

CHAPTER 10
Family, Friends, Fears and Tears

I have been unable to sleep. I realize my boys are up and playing downstairs so I bring their breakfast to eat in front of the television and I turn on my computer. I thought I would continue writing in my journal, but a book that the author claims has cured cancer through the macrobiotic way distracts me. I know my doctor is not a supporter of this diet, but for the next hour I'm on the Internet searching for macrobiotic diets and other alternative therapies via google.com. I get lost in these searches. It is almost an obsession to see what is out there about melanoma. This comes from impatience and a sense of helplessness as I await treatment.

A little while later, Josh comes down with Marsha and for some reason I'm feeling lethargic and depressed. I ask Josh if he could handle the kids so I could get more sleep. He too is exhausted, but he does it and I am able to get the extra hour.

Later on, this becomes a day of comfort for Josh and me. Friends we haven't seen in a while call us up and ask if they could visit. The first callers are friends who happen to be in town from Baltimore.

While they are here, we get a call from the couple who set Josh and me up ten years ago—they happen to be in the area and want to know if they can stop by. When the two couples meet, they realize they are distant cousins who haven't seen each other in years.

Both couples stay a while and manage to lift our spirits. When they leave, we get more visitors. My Aunt Wilma and Uncle Stephen, who live in Manhattan, are passing by because we live close to their summer home in Atlantic Beach and they come to say hello. It's nice to see them, though it's a short visit.

Then I get a call from my friend Jordana who lives in Riverdale, New York. She is in the neighborhood and asks if she can stop by. I start laughing on the phone. I tell her, "Come over, you'll understand." When Jordana arrives, I tell her that she and her family are our fourth set of visitors this day. The irony is that Sundays are usually quiet and uneventful and this Sunday had begun as a depressing one for both Josh and me. Hours later, four different families do the good deed of visiting the sick, which manages to pull Josh and me out of our depressed moods.

How does one account for all these visitors? At these moments I ask God, *"Here you obviously give me all these blessings, but where does the cancer, or the risk of a recurrence, or the loss of half of my foot, and perhaps the inability to have more children fit into the picture? I see the blessings and miracles but don't understand the rest."*

Monday, December 26

Everything is making me cry today.

I began the day by bumping into a friend who has hurt me for some time but I have been unable to express my feelings. She asked me to join her for coffee but today I could not. I could no longer pretend that nothing was bothering me.

I went to Josh's office to write her a letter even though our miscommunications have gone on for over three years. I know she doesn't mean to hurt but she seems oblivious to how her actions make me ache. I am looking for a level of consideration and sensitivity.

Josh hesitated. What was I going to accomplish with this letter?

She wasn't going to change. I have to accept who she is and what her friendship gives me. Yet, I felt it was killing me. I wasn't satisfied with bumping into her now and then, pretending not to feel angry.

The post office happens to be near a children's clothing store and they were having a 50-percent off sale. I called Josh and asked him to pick Zach up from school. Thank God, he came through. Before I went home I dropped off the letter in my friend's mailbox. By the time I came home, I was exhausted and needed to sleep.

I woke up at 4 PM and noticed I had two messages on my machine—both from my friend. She didn't sound angry as I had expected but rather sorry. I called her and we both agreed it wasn't worth rehashing and better to address the hurt I was feeling. I was pleasantly surprised that she acknowledged my feelings without being defensive. We made a time later in the week to talk. This is my last week before Biochemotherapy.

I later took Marsha to the doctor for a follow-up checkup. I began to cry. One of the doctors handed me some tissues and told me it was all right. I told him my treatment was a week away and he said it was okay to be anxious.

I continued crying during the trip home. I put Marsha to bed and then, before running out to meet Josh, at my therapist's office, I treated myself to a frozen yogurt.

I brought the yogurt to the session. When I saw the therapist, I immediately began to cry again. I told her in Josh's presence that since Saturday, I have little patience for my children and the smallest thing makes me cry. In addition, I've told Josh to "take over" as I locked myself in the bathroom.

My therapist acknowledged a two-week to ten-day period before treatment when reality kicks in. The therapist was more concerned about whether Josh was able to deal with me not being present and taking increased responsibility for the kids. Josh's response was, "I love my kids. I've learned to feed and care for them. That doesn't mean I don't want to put a shotgun to my head sometimes!"

It is going to be hard on both of us. I will be sick and out of it and even though his mother will be around, the heaviest burden will be on Josh. We discussed the possibility of his being resentful toward me. He may feel, during and after my treatment, I am not doing my share. We talked about how he might prepare for these reactions.

Thank God I live in this generous community where people cook dinner for me and my family every night. I'm embarrassed that I still need this help considering that I am walking around but when it comes to things unrelated to my treatment, for example, taking care of my husband and children, I just cannot seem to get it together—even putting a shopping list together is a challenge. Yet I know Josh feels comforted and taken care of by the community, as do the kids.

Once again, my therapist validated my feelings. I may seem okay, but if people want to help me then let them—because I am not okay. The truth is that I am spacey. That is why I write down my thoughts, because since surgery I have lacked concentration to follow-through with even the simplest of tasks.

CHAPTER 11
Countdown to Treatment

Meanwhile, I'm thinking about my Biochemotherapy. I think I should pack my bag. The other day I went to buy some comfortable shirts to wear in the hospital because I don't like wearing pajamas all day or—it goes without saying—hospital gowns.

When I was pregnant and about to give birth to each of my children, I would cook and bake and prepare clean baby clothing. When our first was born, Josh slept at the hospital with me. With our second and third we felt it was more important for him to be home.

This time when I was admitted to the hospital, Josh and I were not sure what to do. I wanted Josh with me but, on the other hand, we felt nervous leaving the kids without a parent. Josh fears if he stays home he'll be worrying how I am at the hospital. In the end, we decided he would come up the first two days, go home and come back again for Shabbat. I'll be discharged on Saturday and we have to wait until nightfall to drive home. In the interim, my sister Deborah would be there with me. The hospital has a chair that becomes a cot. Knowing my mother-in-law will be with our children, I am less nervous for Josh to be away for a few days.

I am constantly researching melanoma on the Internet. I come across an article that describes the side effects of Biochemo. Just reading the description makes me want to throw up. I showed Josh the list and tears welled in his eyes with compassion and pain. Here is the list:

<u>Most Common Toxic Effects of Biochemotherapy</u>

Toxicity	Description
Constitutional:	Fever, chills, malaise, mylagia
Hematological:	Anemia, neutropenia, thrombocytopenia
Gastrointestinal:	Anorexia, nausea, vomiting, diarrhea, elevation of liver function tests.
Cardiovascular:	Hypotension, arrhythmia, congestive heart failure
Renal and Electrolyte:	Increased creatinine, hypomagnesemia, hyponatremia
Infection:	Catheter-related, neutropenic fever, oral candidiasis
Cutaneous/mucosal:	Skin rash, oral pharyngitis, alopecia, vitiligo
Endocrine:	Hyper- or hypothyroidism
Neurological:	Peripheral neuropathy, depression, insomnia, latency, and cognitive changes.

Even if I cannot understand all the medical terms, it still scares the hell out of me. I had not realized the treatment would be this toxic but, if this is going to give me the chance to live a longer life, and perhaps even cure me of this crazy disease, then I have to stay focused and accept that this is the treatment for me.

Someone suggested that I buy a small tape recorder for the hospital at moments when I may feel too weak to write. I found a Dictaphone on the Internet and I am also trying to prepare some books on tape. Will I be awake? Will I be lucid? I have no idea about anything and certainly no idea what I will do with myself all day.

I am not enthusiastic about praying to God in our ancient Hebrew words, but want to establish a connection beforehand so when I'm in the hospital my channel to God will be clear. I always find comfort in this Psalm:

Psalm 23

A psalm for David: Hashem (God) is my shepherd, I shall not lack. In lush meadows He lays me down, beside tranquil waters He leads me. He restores my soul. He leads me on paths of righteousness for His Name's sake. Though I walk in the valley overshadowed by death, I will fear no evil, for you are with me. Your rod and your staff, they comfort me. You prepare a table before me in full view of my tormentors. You anointed my head with oil, my cup overflows. May only goodness and kindness pursue me all the days of my life, and I shall dwell in the House of Hashem for long days. (ArtScroll)

Thursday, January 1, 2004

It is 1:00 PM and both of Josh's parents are now with us from Montreal.

Friday, January 2

I have physical therapy at 9:30 AM. and I get home in time for a scheduled massage. During the massage, my in-laws come back from shopping with Ozzie. When Ozzie comes upstairs, I hear him call "Mommy, mommy, I want my mommy." As those familiar words ring in my head, I try to block them out to enjoy the massage. Cancer or no cancer, it is hard not to feel guilty.

I organize my clothing for the hospital. I put aside some books and CDs. I rent books on CD from the public library. I'm contemplating whether to take my yoga mat, because I have another tape with a 15-minute session, but have no idea how I am going to feel at the hospital.

Tonight's Shabbat meal is beautiful even though Josh and his father go out to eat at a local *bar mitzvah* dinner. Norma and I stay home and eat with the kids. We are singing Shabbat songs. The kids join in and dance.

When I was a child growing up, my father stressed the "modern" in Modern Orthodoxy. Rituals were practiced but not sacred. The situation got worse when he remarried. At first I enjoyed my new non-religious life. Until that point, I used to be frustrated as to why I could not do my homework on Shabbat while my father smoked his cigarettes. Later I adopted many rituals on my own. Initially my siblings thought I had been brainwashed through a high school seminar. I remember Caroline asking me, "How can you enjoy Friday nights when Friday night dinner in our house is hell!" She was right about that. It was the one day a week when everyone remained at the table a little longer than fifteen minutes. Usually if my father was in a mood, it did not take much to set him off on each one of us.

I remember an incident one Friday night when, for whatever reason, he was yelling at me through the entire meal. When he decided the meal was over, he would say it is time to *bentch* (Yiddish for Grace after a meal). In our home, it was customary for the children to line up after bentching for our father's bracha (blessing). When we were young, Deborah and I would fight over who would get the bracha first. The evening when he was yelling at me, apparently for no reason at all, I started to leave the dining room. My father said, "what about your bracha?" I said, "No thanks," and went straight to my room. I was scared that it would make the situation worse for me. Instead my father laughed and called me "a crybaby and a sore loser." So it is fair to say that Judaism was not a positive experience in my home—but something inside me wanted to reclaim, study, nurture and cherish it.

Ironically, today I have become a Judaic studies teacher and am even married to a rabbi.

Despite our upbringing, all of my siblings take tradition and Judaism seriously.

Today Zach was so proud that he was the Shabbat Rabbi. Even with such positive experiences, my boys still complain that they can't watch television or drive somewhere on Shabbat. We realize that one day their observance will be beyond our control, but we hope our children will follow the paths on which we are trying to lead them.

I feel God has given me so much. I hope that our children too will learn to witness and appreciate the greatness of God.

Early Sunday Morning, January 4

Once again I wake up at 5:00 AM. but, since it is Shabbat, I cannot type. I sit on the living room couch twiddling my thumbs, waiting for one of my children to wake up.

In synagogue, at the bar mitzvah of twin boys my husband had taught, I get such comments as, "It's so nice to see you getting out." and, "you look great!" Of course these comments are well intentioned but *what am I supposed to look like?*

I tell Zach I am leaving for the hospital tomorrow. Up until now, my kids think I have recovered — but I've only recovered from foot surgery. Now I am going to be sick again for the next three months and it will be hard for them.

Sunday Continued, January 4th

I wake up this morning in a better mood. It's a good sign that I was able to sleep to 6:30 AM. Today is *Asarah b'Tevet*. After the fast day, Josh and I will go to Atlantic City for the night. First, it's a much shorter drive to Philadelphia than it is from Long Island. Second, Josh likes to play Black Jack and I like the slot machines. It will be a welcomed distraction as I prepare for my first treatment tomorrow.

I spend the rest of the day getting last minute things together, including packages to send Zach and Ozzie so they will think I sent them from the hospital. In each package is a little Matchbox car, just enough to say I am thinking of them.

Then I thought of a great idea — to get the kids dressed and ready for the mall so I could take pictures of them with me to the hospital. Norma and I took the pictures and the children behaved well, even though it took an hour to develop the pictures. I know I will enjoy them in the hospital.

It's bedtime. I have told Zach I will be leaving for the hospital but have not told Ozzie yet. I am not sure what a three-year-old child understands or needs to understand. I finish reading Ozzie a book and tell him, "I'm going away, but Tata (*Savta* — grandma) and *Sabba* (grandpa) are here." Ozzie started to whine. I am not sure what he understands but he uses the opportunity to ask me, "Mommy, one more book?" Ozzie chooses his book, *The Mommy Book*, and then Zach wants another book and he chooses *The Hug*. Both of their book choices make me smile. I read them the books and then I kiss and hug them goodnight. Just the other day I had taught Zach how to do Eskimo kisses and butterfly kisses. He asks me before I leave the room, "Can I give you a butterfly kiss?" My heart melts, and I say, "Of course."

Hours later, I am sitting in the hotel room and Josh is already touring the game tables downstairs. I choose to do a twenty-minute yoga workout to help calm myself down before I meet the slot machines. I am trying to keep my mind healthy even though I know the Biochemotherapy is going to attack my body.

As opposed to earlier in the week when I was crying all the time, tonight I am actually in a good mood. I feel pumped. I feel ready for the treatment. I feel ready to start it and strong enough to get through it.

Monday, January 5th

Today is the day I go into the hospital. I am glad we came to the casino last night because instead of using my nervous energy at home to clean more closets I played the slots, which was a good distraction. I actually won one hundred dollars which is just enough to pay for my massage at the casino's spa before we leave for Philadelphia. As the hour gets closer to the massage time, I open my prayer book and make sure to pray with extra concentration.

I had requested a wake up call at 7:45 AM. so I could make it to my massage on time, which was really wishful thinking on my part. I had gone to sleep at 2 AM and was up and ready to go at 6:30 AM. I definitely felt anxious so I took a valium and listened to a meditation tape to help me relax.

In July of 2002, my feelings toward prayer changed. When I was pregnant with Marsha many women and men were praying from the Book of Psalms for my recovery from melanoma. Since then I believe that God was listening to all those who prayed for me.

The Hebrew prayer book has been a challenge for me ever since my father died. Prior to his death, I would run to pray the morning and afternoon services. I enjoyed the time I was able to set aside each day to focus on my relationship with God and show my appreciation.

When my father died, I took upon myself the practice of saying "Mourner's *Kaddish*," a prayer recited three times a day in honor of the dead. Even though the relationship with my father had failed in my eyes, I wanted to treat his memory with respect as children are required to honor their parents, whether living or deceased.

My recitation of the *Kaddish* began as an uplifting experience but the feeling slowly deteriorated with the reaction of some men to my recitation. In the Orthodox world, the prayer of *Kaddish* is a man's obligation, but I knew that it was permissible for a woman to also recite the prayer even though it was not frequently done. When I had attended services at Barnard-Columbia, certain men would leave the service as I said my *Kaddish* and return when it was completed. Initially, I tried not to let it bother me because the prayer of *Kaddish* has nothing really to do with the dead. It is about the living left behind and their declaration of belief in God's ways. How could an innocent prayer be such a problem? Didn't these people realize I was mourning a loss and the act was an act of sorrow rather than feminism? Gradually, the departure of such people during my *Kaddish* began to affect me and each time I cried. As the eleven months ended, I only had courage to show up for services once a day.

The *Kaddish* experience distanced me from our holy prayer book. During the years that followed, it was a challenge to pray from it. I no longer related to the words I knew by heart. I was praying by rote, without feeling.

Since my first experience with melanoma, I have tried to reconnect spiritually with the prayer book but it is difficult. The funny thing is that I am usually talking to God all day, but in my own words. I constantly thank God for His goodness to me and my family.

Yet recently, and particularly as I was awaiting my second diagnosis, I found myself crying the whole time I was driving to work. When I came to work, I decided to join in one of the prayer services instead of pray by myself and this gave me comfort.

Belief, faith, and spirituality are not stagnant. God gave us commandments to become better people. I think I have to keep trying to find outlets for religious expression, whether through prayer, study, charity, working with the sick, or baking *challah* (bread eaten on

Shabbat). Better to focus on people in need of help than on my own predicament, which is beyond my control anyway.

We are on our way to the hospital. We finally arrive and I am sitting in a crowded admissions room. There must be at least 100 people waiting to be admitted. From admissions, I go to Interventional Radiology where a pick will be placed in my arm for the Chemotherapy drugs. Later I will have a different line put in for the Biological drugs.

Now we are sitting in Radiology and my Aunt Wilma, one of my mother's sisters, meets me there. She had taken the train from Manhattan in order to care for me during my first few days of treatment. She sees me writing and asks, "What are you writing about?" I think it would be painful for her to hear about my topic as both she and my Aunt Gail, another of my mother's sisters, are breast cancer survivors. I know my Aunt Wilma had always been at my mother's sickbed, caring for her.

I tell Aunt Wilma that the theme of my book is *trying to correct the mistakes of my parents*. Her first reaction is a little defensive: "Things were different then. No one even spoke about cancer!" I explain that I am writing about my search for a female role model. My aunt responds, "You don't even realize how much you are like your mother in personality, practice of religion, social qualities, and leadership skills." As I listen, I also reflect on the fact that my mother and I share a similar reason for living, *our children.*

I reply to my aunt, "That is unfortunately my whole point. Those are your memories and not mine. I'm not denying that my mother influenced my first six years of life; I'm just frustrated that I don't remember and have to rely on other people's memories. Wouldn't it be the same if, God forbid, something should happen to me? My children are too young to remember me and how I influenced their early years of life."

Aunt Wilma answers, "But your situation is not your mother's situation. If something should happen to you, your children would have the benefit of family support which you didn't have as a child." After my mother had passed away, my father would not allow us to speak to her parents and her sisters. It was only when I was eighteen that I reached out to my aunts and grandmother to establish my own relationships with them.

I say, "That's exactly my point. I have the opportunity now to ensure that my children's experiences will not be mine whether I live or die. That is why I have been doing all this planning and meeting with professionals, something my father never did."

Then my aunt had tears in her eyes and I began to understand her feelings. She told me she had difficulty sleeping last night. I remembered that when my mother was ill, Aunt Wilma had always been there with her in the hospital and now even though things are a little different with me, it brings painful flashbacks. There is an element of greater pain because now she is taking the sick daughter of her late, beloved sick sister to begin her cancer treatment.

I finally get called to see the radiologist and he explains the procedure they are about to do. He asks me, "Do you have any questions?"

I say, "Yes, when can we start?"

The doctor asks, "Are you in a rush?"

Keeping in mind the fact that we had already been waiting in the hospital for four hours, I tell him, "I have twelve DVDs that I would like to start watching. I also would like to eat something before I lose my appetite for two weeks."

The doctor is taken aback. I apologize for my dark humor and he responds very nicely, "I feel bad that you have to go through this."

"Thanks," I answer.

There is still a wait to get into another room where the radiologist will put the pick in. I feel tired, but cannot sleep. I use the time to write postcards to Zachary, Ozzie, and Marsha with cool stickers on them.

It takes the radiologist a few tries to get the pick in. Finally he has to call in the attending radiologist to do the job, but in the interim we schmooze. He tells me how he used to be a teacher for "Teach America." It was teaching amongst the population of urban areas that made him decide to be a doctor. He says he was working with urban children who were not receiving quality medical care and so his goal is to help the urban community.

I am so impressed that I tell him that I too had wanted to become a doctor. As a child I imagined finding a cure for breast cancer. It wasn't until I was about seventeen before I understood that my desire to be a doctor was related to my mother's death and stemmed from a feeling of helplessness. I then realized that what I liked most about being a doctor was the ability to help people. I chose to be a high school teacher because as many teachers know, high school is not just about communicating knowledge, but also to impart skills to the students that will help them cope with life's challenges. I teach Jewish History and Bible, but I simultaneously teach manners, limits and boundaries, respect, and how to deal with disappointment and stress.

It is 5:30 PM. and I am finally in a room. I had been told that my doctor was not supposed to stop by until tomorrow but she comes to say hello anyway, which is very comforting. She explains that my medications will probably begin close to midnight and apologizes that being in the hospital is not going to be a place where I will be getting a lot of sleep.

Then an old friend stops by with her husband who is a resident in the hospital. She makes Josh and me dinner. It is so nice to see her, especially since we had lost touch for many years. When she heard I was coming to the hospital she made an effort to come and see me despite the time that had elapsed.

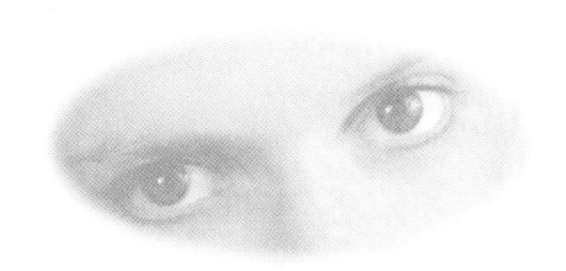

CHAPTER 12
Let the Battle Begin!

Tuesday, January 6

I made it through my first night!

The nurses began the Interleukin-2 infusion and interferon at 10 PM. At 11 PM, they put the DTIC, Cisplastin, and Vinblastine through my pick. I slept well from 10 PM to 2 AM and then the side effects crept in. I had nausea, the sweats, stiff and cramping legs and lower back pain.

The cramping was probably a reaction to the interferon, which brings on flu-like symptoms. The nausea was expected, but the anti-nausea medicine wasn't helping. The nurse then offered me an alternative nausea medication called Compazin. With this drug I actually began to hallucinate. I began imagining that Aunt Wilma was asking me questions and I answered even when I realized no one was talking to me. (she slept in my room the first night) We ended up taking a walk around the ward. Then I sat in a chair for a while because lying down was making the nausea worse. In addition to the other medications, I was given Tylenol and Naprocin to take care of the aches, pains, and temperature. I was also taking Keflex as a prophylactic antibiotic because of my low white cell blood count.

I am tired but doing well. The doctor had stopped by this morning and was pleasantly surprised. She said it would probably remain this way until the evening when I get my next Biochemotherapy medication.

I told the doctor I had used meditation and Yoga for two months before the treatment as preparation for this battle. I felt too embarrassed to mention the prayers.

Despite my tiredness, I did a fifteen-minute yoga workout. It was a good workout and even Aunt Wilma joined me. Lacking part of my right foot, I can only do the yoga stretching and not the stances.

Some time later Josh just came in. He slept at a nearby apartment last night because,

1. I did not want him to get scared from the side effects and
2. I thought it would be good for him to get some rest.

The *Bikur Cholim*, the Jewish organization that takes care of the sick in Philadelphia, has been generous in providing my family lodging and food.

I put together more care packages for Zach and Ozzie to show them they are not out of my mind. This time I sent Matchbox airplanes.

Then Josh told me what I had missed yesterday at home. Marsha fell and chipped a wedge in both her front teeth. My mother-in-law had to take her to the dentist without us. Marsha is okay, but Josh and I were shaken up to have been away from our little baby.

I slept most of the day without nausea, but the Interlukin-2 was making me tired.

I'm tired and lack the energy to maintain a conversation, but appreciate phone calls anyway.

Deborah brought Godiva chocolates, my favorite treats—except the cherry and the coconut ones. My doctor had warned me not to eat my favorite foods during treatment because it might cause aversions to them. She was right. I could not eat one chocolate and gave the box to the doctor who told me that she too loves Godivas.

A stranger stopped by today while I was sleeping and left me this note:

"…I went through Chemo last year and I am still getting treatments. Wednesdays are my day so maybe I can stop in tomorrow after mine…. Now I can pray for you with your face in mind. I will get your Hebrew name…. Please call me if you need anything."

I never met the person who wrote that letter but it gave me comfort.

I showered this evening because I had the sweats from the night before, and I wanted to feel clean before the nurse started up my medications again. It was a little complicated to remove all the wires, but the shower felt humanizing, especially being able to put on fresh underwear and clothing. It helped me feel refreshed in the sanitized and stale hospital environment.

I spoke on the phone with Zach, who thanked me for the Matchbox cars. He was so excited about getting mail that, in return, he wanted to send me some pictures he had drawn.

Sending my children packages is one of many ways I could make a correction based on my own childhood experience. I have had time to prepare in advance for my treatment and I knew my children would love to get mail. I miss them and would never want them to feel I stopped thinking about them. I sent them Matchbox airplanes today, present number three. They should arrive by Friday. I miss Zach's kisses, Ozzie's hugs, and Marsha's asserting her little self by saying, "No."

Wednesday, January 7

Deborah told me she was feeling a lot of anxiety watching my skin color turn bright red, which is a reaction to the Interlukin-2. She slept in my room last night, and I slept through the night with no side effects but woke early with a sore neck and lower back. I used hot packs for the pain and now I have a headache — not yet as bad as I had anticipated. I watched television for a bit and then fell asleep again.

I am growing disappointed with the nursing staff. The first night, the nurse had been so on top of everything that my husband said in awe, "Hospitals have little to do with the doctors. It's the nursing staff that carries the floor." The second night, the nurse was terrible. I had to wait twenty minutes each time I rang for her. I should have received a Tylenol at 5 AM when my aches and pains were already setting in but at 5:30 AM I was still buzzing the nurse. At 8:30 AM, I had to introduce myself to the morning nurse and tell her it was almost time for my Tylenol. It's frustrating.

I received a phone call from a co-worker for whom I have the utmost respect. When I heard her voice, I began to cry. I could not believe she had made time to think of me when she works full-time, has a household of five children, and takes on responsibilities as the wife of a high school principal. I felt honored and comforted by her call.

I had a panic attack. My intravenous pump started beeping for the twentieth time today and no nurse answered my ring. I got myself out of bed and began walking down the hall of the hospital ward looking for someone to help me.

I slept most of the day. Josh went home to be with the kids. Deborah will stay until Friday unless Pamela gives birth sooner.

I asked myself if I should call my psychiatrist. One side effect of interferon is depression and I am starting to feel down and weepy. I wonder if this is depression. I wait for my oncologist to stop by before I make the call.

Then my doctor came by and I was so happy to see her. It's important to feel comfortable with your doctor and she fits the bill. She looked at me and, with a smile, said how impressed she was at the way I was handling the treatment. I talked it over with my sister and the nurse practitioner on the floor. They both said it was normal to feel weepy during treatment—being here all day, inactive and not much to do.

My sister offered to give me a massage and it was so called for! Then she wanted me to get up and go to the cafeteria with her because the kosher frozen food I had been receiving was horrible. As we zigzagged through the hospital, the nurses seemed impressed that I was walking around. People with my treatment usually do not get out of bed. But one nurse stopped me and said I can't just go to the cafeteria with a chemo monitor. She said, "What happens if it should spill and get onto someone's skin?"

So I said, "It is okay to pump this stuff through my veins, but intolerable for even the slightest drop to fall on someone's skin?"

She said I could go to the cafeteria as long as I had a sign on my monitor that I was a chemo patient. I thought to myself, "*It's not enough to be on a chemo ward for 5 to 6 days, but must I also draw attention to myself with a sign?*"

Later that evening Josh's Hillel Rabbi, from the University of

Pennsylvania, came to visit me. I must have met him once or twice before I began to cry again because I could not believe how many people were out there who wanted to wish me a full recovery.

Deborah went out for dinner and I thought now would be a good time to return phone calls. I was feeling such an emotional mess because everything was triggering my tears. I missed my children even though I would be unable to care for them or even tolerate them now. To some degree, I'm happy to be in Philadelphia as it means I am not overwhelmed with visitors. Even though people mean well, this was not a happy occasion like giving birth to a child. Sometimes I feel that visiting me is almost like paying a shiva call (after someone dies the mourners gather for seven days and receive visitors) and I feel pressure to entertain them because they feel so uncomfortable.

I called my *Consegrity* therapist to tell her she must be doing a good job because my nurses and doctor are impressed that not only am I sitting up and talking, but that I'm walking around as well. I told her I was still having aches and nausea, but was not bedridden.

She said, "This is usually the feedback when we treat patients on Chemo, that the side effects are diminished."

I said to myself, *Thank God the side effects are diminished — I'm not sure how much more I could handle."*

One nurse made my day by finding some raspberry ices because there were no more on my floor. She went to a different floor and came back with four cups of raspberry ices. Now, here is a good nurse! The ices are soothing — I am beginning to develop mouth sores and thrush, another side-effect.

I am tired. Deborah is not back yet. I can't tell whether I am bored, depressed or simply tired.

I miss home. I miss Josh. I am glad Deborah is with me and that she took time away from her family to help me but I still miss my family.

I am going to listen to a meditation tape. Maybe it will help relax me.

Thursday, January 8

I woke up again this morning with terrible body aches especially in my neck and lower back. I also have a sore throat. I have been using Nystatin to treat the mouth sores.

Today I was troubled about *Consegrity* and the macrobiotic diet. Both make the individual responsible for his illness by means of energy flow and diet. However, it seems that my health is beyond my control. I can only try the best I can to prevent another cancer, but there are no guarantees for any treatment—conventional or alternative.

I then did a yoga workout, which actually helped my back. Oops! My intravenous for the Interlukin-2 fell out. It only takes the nurse four jabs at my arm before she gets it back in. It's annoying to be in the hospital. You can ask a nurse a question and she answers you, and then hours later you bring up the discussion again and she has no recollection.

It has been hard to dress modestly in the hospital because a long-sleeved shirt causes problems in the wires. I end up wearing a sports tank top to avoid any beeping, but get embarrassed when a religious person visits. I have to ask him to wait outside until I put on a robe and a hair covering. Sometimes I feel, in these hospital situations, that anything goes. Sometimes I cannot get to my robe and hat fast enough, so what should I be doing? I don't intend to make men feel uncomfortable. It is also hard to wear a hat all day when I'm cooped up in the hospital.

I feel bad to say I'm relieved not to have many visitors, even though I had enjoyed the company in New York after foot surgery. I still felt pressure to be funny and entertaining. The narcotics I was taking as pain relief must have kept me interesting to observe, as I was hallucinating. Now under Biochemotherapy I feel so ill that I cannot handle the pressure of entertaining. I just need a lot of quiet time.

Tomorrow Deborah leaves for New York. Josh will come for Shabbat and then he will take me home.

I'm so constipated that my stomach is killing me; apparently that's another side-effect. Then, on the seventh to tenth day following the beginning of my treatment I'm supposed to expect diarrhea.

The good news is that tonight is my last Biochemo infusion, but I have to stay another 24 hours because the Interulukin-2 isn't finished. I can't believe my first treatment is almost finished after all the anxiety buildup. I'll have to see how I feel when I get home because the side effects are still supposed to be present, if not worse.

Friday, January 9

I had a long and uncomfortable night—not from the Biochemo, but from the nurses and aides who would not let me sleep. Every few hours there was poking to put more medicine in my pick, or more blood was drawn, or they woke me for Tylenol.

I had already started packing even though I'm not leaving until tomorrow. I am eager to get home to my family and my bed. The days have gone by so slowly. I still have two more rounds of this with three weeks between each treatment.

I have confidence in Norma and know that she and Josh are taking great care of the kids, but still wonder and fear how my children will greet me when I come home. *Will Zach be sad? Will Ozzie be angry? Will Marsha even notice?* On the other hand, my children are capable of tackling me as soon as they see me. We will just have to see.

I haven't had much time to talk about this hospital stay. I just had to stay focused and get through it. Whatever I expected, the worst did not happen. While waiting for my right foot to heal, anxiety over the upcoming Biochemotherapy in Philadelphia had been more emotionally draining than the actual treatment and hospital stay. Had I gone straight from surgery to treatment in Philadelphia, I would not have had time to think and worry. As it was, the two-month waiting period drove me crazy. I'm sure it drove Josh crazy as well.

Saturday night, January 10

This has been the longest day of my life. Had Josh and I not been Shabbat observers we could have checked out this morning. Instead, we had to wait until Shabbat was over. This morning the intravenous for the Interlukin-2 fell out once again. The nurse had difficulty finding a good vein so they called the doctor, who said to finish the treatment even though I had a few hours left. Meanwhile I still have this pick in my arm and I have to wait until I am discharged (which means after Shabbat) for the nurse practitioner to remove it. I just want to be intravenous-free already. Both the hospital staff and the doctor have been friendly, but it's *time to go home*!

When I told friends and family I was going for treatment outside of New York, many responded, *"What! Can't you get this treatment in New York?"* When you live in New York City, you have a hard time believing it's not the center of the universe. I tried asking oncologists in New York if they could follow the Biochemotherapy protocol, but once I read about the side effects I wanted to be in a hospital with an experienced oncologist in this treatment and an experienced nursing staff. Now that my first treatment is over, I have a skin rash that itches like hell, and the mouth sores are spreading to my throat. Besides these side effects, everything has been bearable. I think I got myself too worked up in preparation for the treatment because I had no idea what to expect and expected the worst.

When the doctor came to say goodbye she said, "Whenever I come into this room I feel a sense of peace." I took that as a compliment.

I have to find the courage to go through two more treatments. The next treatment will be three weeks away. For the first two weeks that I am home, I need to get blood drawn twice a week to check my white blood cell counts and platelets.

Sunday, January 11th

We arrived late last night, after my children's bedtime, but I made sure to peek in and give each child a kiss. The only things I tried to eat were toast and tea, but even the tea bothered my mouth sores. I slept the first few hours of the night, and woke up at 4 AM. I tried taking a valium, but it didn't help.

Why am I so nervous? Is it being home? I want to be home. Am I scared that someone is going to get me sick and that I might have to go the hospital? Unfortunately, my children and their friends are Petri dishes for viral and bacterial growth. Maybe I am just eager to see my kids!

I am hungry so I will try to eat breakfast presently. A little later, Zach wakes up and says, "Mommy, you're here! I love you, mommy."

My heart was melting because he is not always that affectionate, so of course I told him, "I love you too."

His reply, "I love you from the ground to the ceiling."

And mine, "I love you from the back door to the front door," started him giggling.

And then he said, "That's silly, mommy!"

I am so happy to be home. I cannot wait to see Marsha and Ozzie's reactions. Then Ozzie wakes up. He runs screaming to me, "Mommy, mommy!"

Marsha too wakes up and toddles in saying, "Mommy, mommy." I really feel loved.

Apart from the pleasure of my morning greetings, I feel completely listless. I did not anticipate feeling worse than I had at the hospital but didn't have the strength to pick up the children to hug them—and Marsha's only 23 pounds.

I can walk and when I am walking I feel fine, but the minute I exert any energy, whether it's assembling a toy or picking up Marsha, I'm exhausted and have to go to sleep. It makes me wonder if my mother had been strong enough to hold me.

Besides being sent home to rest, I have to give myself four shots this week. The first is called Neulasta and that is supposed to boost my white blood cell count. The next shots are interferon which must be injected on Monday, Wednesday, and Friday, a continuation of my Biological treatment from the hospital, which should add to whatever side effects I am already feeling.

I was able to give the shots to myself after a doctor showed me how to inject the interferon. I'm used to giving myself shots because I self-inject with Imitrex when I get migraine headaches. The experience is not so bad. You just grab a chunk of fat from your thigh, put in the needle, and it's over and painless.

Thank God, Norma is here and we just hired a college student to work the afternoons from 4 PM – 7 PM as well as Sundays. I like my college helper especially because she had been my student two years ago and we are comfortable with each other. She is awesome with kids. She goes right to work and does not rely on instructions. She knows how to fill in where my kids are lacking. She plays with them, takes them to after-school activities, helps with dinner, and even gives them a bath and puts on their pajamas.

The moment I try to help Norma and Rachel I have no energy. Even writing down my feelings wipes me out.

As I'm sitting here writing, Norma and Josh are bathing my children. It's cute to hear them play. If only I could give them a bath! I sometimes feel like an interloper in my own home.

Tuesday, January 13

It surprised me how little I was able to write yesterday. I hadn't anticipated that I would feel so weak and nauseous at home. I forced myself to drink a healthy shake for breakfast and then eat a scrambled egg for lunch. I couldn't finish it, but Marsha was happy to do so. My taste buds are unable to taste anything.

I'm in shock at how hard the treatment is hitting me at home. At the hospital everyone was telling me how great I was, and I wasn't prepared to stay in bed all day. In the past when I have felt sick I could still run around and distract myself. I didn't feel quarantined. Now, I just don't feel like moving. The smallest effort, like unscrewing a bottle, makes me exhausted.

I went today to have my blood work taken. The nurse asked in a concerned way, "Are you okay? Is there someone here who will drive you home?" I didn't realize how much exhaustion was written on my face.

Rachel has plenty of energy for my kids. I must have interviewed so many people, but I hadn't needed another babysitter/housekeeper. I needed someone to play with my children when I was unable. The fact that Rachel is working out well feels like a miracle. She comes when I need her, when the boys are a little wild and tired from a full day at school.

Simone, my massage therapist, arrived and started to work. I told her that when a friend calls and asks how I'm feeling, I'm not sure what she wants to hear. Sometimes I feel pressured to say I'm feeling good because it makes her feel better. Other times, when I tell a friend I'm feeling sick, I feel by her silence over the phone that she doesn't know how to respond.

Simone says, "Why don't you just tell them the truth?"

"What do you mean the truth?"

"When you are having a good day just say, 'I'm a having a good day and my spirits are high even though it's a difficult time,' and then if you're having a bad day just tell the person, 'I appreciate your call, but I'm not feeling so well at the moment.'"

I am in awe at how simply Simone is able to discuss "the truth." Usually when I feel well, I take that as a reason to run away from the fact that I'm being treated for cancer. But now, focusing on "the truth" helps me maintain awareness of this difficult time and acknowledge how I'm feeling.

My sister Deborah asks me how the kids are doing. I tell her that, with Norma and Rachel helping them, they are doing well — almost as if they are not feeling the changes going on. My sister responds bluntly, "I'm sure they feel the changes."

When I get off the phone, my sister's statement sticks with me and upsets me. I know she is telling me the truth, but it's still so hard to hear. I don't want hear reality, fantasy is good for now. On the one hand I feel, *don't burst my bubble.* On the other hand, her statement penetrates because I feel guilty to be ruining my children's lives by giving them the same pain I lived with as a child of a sick and dying mother.

Today Ozzie pointed to my right, bare foot and said, "Mommy, there's your boo-boo?" I know Zach understands a lot more than Ozzie. I wish I could always protect them both.

CHAPTER 13

New Beginnings

Wednesday, January 14

I woke up with a little more energy today. I began my day by giving away a lot of Zach and Ozzie's clothing. I used to keep everything in boxes, but then felt it's better for someone who needs it to use it now than for the clothing to sit in storage. I also donated my wedding dress.

I then felt strong enough to go on an errand. Our dishwasher had broken down and Norma I went shopping for a replacement. Since Josh and I have been married, we spent one year, when we lived in Israel without a dishwasher. Could I clean my own plate? Yes. Do I want to? No. I also purchased a separate freezer because we freeze a lot of food for the kids. I am aspiring to be like my friend, a radiologist and neighbor. On Sundays, she shops and organizes five precooked meals that she places in the freezer. In the morning, she takes out one tray to thaw by the time she gets home from work, and bakes it. I consider that super organized.

Before I became sick, Josh and I ate pasta, take-out and pizza. Then, after my surgery, volunteers from the community began to cook for us each day, including Shabbat. The funny thing is that Josh has gained weight over this period. These meals were not merely pasta. Sometimes there were appetizers, and usually a salad, meat, vegetable, starch, and occasionally freshly baked cookies for dessert. I am grateful to my friend Esti, who would call me every day or so to ask if I needed food. She organized the whole production.

I feel guilty I am not a good housewife. Even though I work full-time too, I feel bad when Josh hears from other wives how they prepare dinner for their husbands every night. Apart from guilt, I think it would be good to be more proactive about our food choices.

Tomorrow I go for another blood test. I had received good results from my Monday test, even though I was feeling weak, and hope to get good news again from tomorrow's test—especially because I'm feeling stronger. Monday I was barely able to move, and today I had to tell myself to stop and do less.

Thursday, January 15

Today, for many reasons, I began my day stressed. I needed to get myself to the diagnostic lab to be blood tested and there was a snowstorm outside. I keep calling the lab to see if it's open, but I just get an answering machine. Then I'm nervous that the doctor might suggest I come back after two weeks instead of three. The problem with that possibility is that Norma will not be here to help with my kids if I go in two weeks. She has to be in Boston to deliver lectures and then back to Montreal for a few days. If I go to the hospital in two weeks, Josh can't take me. Nevertheless, I convince myself that Biochemo on a 21-day cycle instead of a 28 day cycle would be more effective. Then I ask myself, "Why am I trying to bring more stress into a stressful situation?"

I get in touch with my doctor and she says people need the 28-day cycle to build up their blood counts and feel stronger. She doesn't think it would be a big deal to wait the three weeks, especially with Norma back. Okay the decision is made, I will wait for Norma and that's one stress off my shoulders.

Then I had a meeting with my psychiatrist and discussed my need for nesting. I've been going through the whole house and allocating things to different charities. What most concerned Josh about my spring-cleaning was that I also wanted to give away the baby toys — a swing, a bouncy seat, a double stroller, and a crib. I tried explaining to Josh that we cannot have more children for at least three years or possibly ever. Why should we keep these things in our garage when someone in need can use them now?

I explained to my psychiatrist, as I had earlier explained to Josh, that I used to keep everything as if I was going to create a documentary of my life one day for my future children. In my imagination, I wanted my children to know everything about me. I kept all the books I had read because they also became part of my experience.

When my father and stepmother were moving to Israel, my stepmother said I could fill up one large box and the rest of my things would have to be thrown out. I cried in my room because to make the decision about what would go and what would stay was so difficult for me. I was concerned that I would have nothing of my childhood to one day share with my own children. I chose to put in the box all my athletic trophies and my varsity basketball jacket to show my children how athletic I had been — especially since now I cannot run around anymore. I also put in some pictures and some memorable essays I had written over the years.

A few months later, when I was studying in Israel and my stepmother and father also lived in Israel, I asked my stepmother about the box because I knew all the boxes had arrived from New York. She said to me — as if I was bothering her — "What box?"

I took a deep gulp of air, trying to hold in my tears. I said, "The box that I put all my stuff in."

She said, "I don't know what you're talking about." I felt she had dismissed my feelings. I was already depressed because she and my father were constantly fighting and now I had no home. Their house in Israel, which my father had built with my mother, could not be a comforting place for me. I wanted to go back to school and forget what had happened. I mourned my lost items for a while but eventually became desensitized to the ownership of material items. I still wanted things, but no longer felt I had to hold onto them forever.

Two years later, after my father died and my stepmother was going through the house, she said to me, "You must come by and pick up all your stuff."

I said, "What stuff?"

She said, "Your trophies and things—you know, the things that you packed up in a box when we left New York."

I was stupefied. I said to her, "I thought you told me that the box was lost a few years ago."

My stepmother replied, with an annoyed inflection in her tone of voice, "I don't know what you're talking about, but if you want your things they are in the basement."

When I arrived at her home (the home was in her name and the only valuable item left in my father's estate), I looked for the box in the basement and it wasn't hard to find. I looked through the box and I realized it must have been there all along, but she lacked the patience and sensitivity to go and look for it. After looking at some trophies and pictures, I put everything back in the box and left the basement. I told her I did not want those things anymore. I felt hurt—first when I had been limited to pack one box and then later to find out the box was gone. I felt they didn't matter anymore. I had emotionally detached from my belongings. That took place more than ten years ago. Now that I have three children, I would like to show them these things but am no longer in touch with my stepmother.

As I'm explaining to my psychiatrist this history of detachment from personal items and present desire to give them away in a meritorious act, he says, "Or it could be understood that you are preparing to die and that could be why Josh is sensitive to your giving away all these things."

I was silent as I pondered that statement and then I said to him, "No, it's the opposite. I want to live so I am taking ownership of my house; I'm hanging pictures on the wall and putting pictures of my family around the house. I think the idea of planning to die is not in my consciousness. If anything, after four years I am finally moving into my house. I, the homeless child, who cared for no material items, has finally stuck her feet in the ground and said, "This is *my* home and this is where I will continue to live!"

My psychiatrist validated my need to organize and give my things to charities. I explained to him that feeling helpless with cancer had made me want to do good deeds for others.

I discussed another issue with my psychiatrist that I have been feeling guilty about—the possibility that one day, because of my illness, our children may need therapy. I asked him, "How would you feel, both as a psychiatrist and a parent, if one of your children needed therapy? Would it feel like you failed them while you were providing therapy for others?"

He answered, "My whole family goes or has gone to therapy. I look at those kids who receive therapy when they are young as lucky because they are being treated when the problem arises. I would not have to treat them later as messed-up adults who can't seem to figure themselves out. I wish these adults had undergone therapy as children!"

Friday, January 16

My sister Caroline flew in this morning from Los Angeles for the birth of Samantha to Pamela and Douglas, who were doing something special to mark the occasion in synagogue on Saturday. It was understood I would not be attending, only a week after treatment, feeling weak, and not wanting to compromise my immune system by being around many people. Caroline flew into John F. Kennedy airport, which is right near my house. She came to visit me early Friday morning before heading for the city.

Caroline, Norma, and I went to an early lunch. I asked Caroline about our mother. At thirteen years when our mother died, Caroline's memories are much more comprehensive than mine. I was saying, "I can imagine how difficult it must have been for mommy to have patience and strength for us."

Caroline answered, "I have memories of mommy before she got sick. I distinctly remember mommy talking to you as if you were older than you were and not 'baby-talking'. She wanted you to be strong and independent."

I thought to myself, "I wish I could have been 'babied' by at least someone." But instead I said, "Where does this notion come from that mommy detach herself from us because she knew she was dying?" I asked because I felt under constant scrutiny that any time I would pull back or need a break, it must mean: Julie's preparing to die and we need to tell her how it is being perceived. I explained that Josh was fearful of my pulling away at times, when in reality these were coping strategies to keep living. I said, "It just occurred to me why I might be so distracted. I have been suffering, not just from childhood traumas, but also from a second diagnosis of melanoma, a partial amputation of my foot, the search for treatment of a disease that has no cure, wondering if I will live or die, and worry over who will watch my children while I undergo treatment. Yes, some of these things have been worked out by now, but I think considering the situation it would be odd if I wasn't trying to escape my loaded reality."

I believe that both Caroline and Norma are sympathetic to my self-preoccupation and I think Norma understands the reason behind my behaviors. My coping strategies are mechanisms to continue living; they are definitely not a preparation for death.

Caroline then said, "Mommy did make a conscious decision to pull back from us. I believe she thought that by pulling away she was helping us to become independent. She felt she was giving us skills to move on after her death."

When I heard this, I felt sad for my siblings and me who had not found the closeness we needed and deserved from our mommy, who was sick for almost all the first six years of my life and a crucial period in theirs, as well. Then, all of a sudden, I felt happy. Zach had just turned five and, despite my episodes of malignant melanoma, I have never *consciously* pulled back from him or from any of my children. I have already given Zach five years of nurturing, intimacy, and care. It's our baby daughter, Marsha, who ironically parallels my personal history. I already had cancer before she was born but am proud to say we have a bond of love and attachment, even with all my surgeries and treatments. Ozzie just can't get enough of me. Wherever I go, he wants to be with me. Though I may project onto my children the loneliness as child-of-an-unavailable-mother, in fact I am available to them.

Caroline then pointed out to me that, though my mother and I received diagnoses of cancer around the same age and had young children at about the same age, there is a major difference between us. When my mother received her prognosis, she knew her cancer was terminal. She still tried any treatment that she could and never stopped fighting, but knew it would get worse. After my surgery, I had become cancer-free. I only took upon myself a very harsh treatment because the cancer left me with a high risk of recurrence, but that does not mean a death sentence as was the case for our mother.

Belatedly, I have arrived at the conclusion that *I am not my mother*. This may have been obvious to readers and family members but I had feared abandoning my children because I felt I had been abandoned. I hope this cancer episode will be my last and that as my children grow older it will be an even less significant factor in our lives. I need to acknowledge, accept and repeat to myself that I am *not* my mother. I have worked hard to become the best mom and pray that our children will be happy and productive, comfortable and secure in knowing who they are, and that Josh and I will live many years to rejoice at and share in their happiness.

This point of realization that I am not my mother was brought about by writing down my thoughts to keep me company throughout my treatments. I hope this work will bring others hope as it did for me. I finally feel I am going to live and no longer need or want to focus on my mother's illness. I only want to focus on life; thanks to God, I have another chance. As two more treatments loom ahead, I pray to continue with God's help to overcome the obstacles placed in my path, and that He will give me wisdom, strength, and health to continue living.

I know that to be the mother I always wished for myself, I must stay alive and be present for all the rites of passage my children will experience. When my little Marsha looks up at me and says, "Mommy, mommy," I know I am not detached. My children are my life, my joy and gifts from God. They are the greatest blessings I ever had. I continually thank God for allowing me to experience joy and happiness. I thank God who gave Josh and me the opportunity to create a beautiful family and joys that are often denied to others.

Caroline reminded me of something my father used to say but which, over time, I had forgotten. When our father would get into one of his defensive behaviors or manic mood swings, he would say to us, "Your Mother never loved you. She did not have the ability to love you. I am all that you have. If you feel pain it's because you never had a mother—it's not my fault."

I thank God I can be a mother and that Josh has the benefit of far greater understanding and compassion than my father had been able to find within him. I can finally say and firmly believe, *we did it, Josh! We made a family and became the parents we always aspired to be.*

Sunday, March 7, 2004

My three treatments are over. Purim is about happiness and so I dress in costume with my children and give the traditional gifts of food to neighbors and friends. I am grateful to be a little stronger.

Today is bittersweet, however. Just before Shabbat, a doctor, in good health, a friend of ours died suddenly and left behind a wife and three young children similar in age to ours. Josh and I attended the funeral. I could not stop weeping. I ached for all the family members who lost this man at a young age. I ached for the children who lost their daddy and for my friend, his wife, who must raise her three children without their father.

This funeral could have been mine. It could have been Josh left alone to father three children. *Why should I be blessed and another family in pain? Why do I get the chance to live longer?* I humbly accept my good fortune and give thanks.

At the funeral a friend of ours said to Josh, "I guess we need to count our blessings every day." I said under my breath, *No, not every day — we have to count our blessings every minute and every second. God gives and takes away in the blink of an eye!*

Today we cannot mourn because the holiday demands we celebrate how Esther and Mordechai saved the Jews from death at the hands of Haman-the-evil. The Jews as a people have survived again.

Josh and I invited all our siblings, their spouses and kids in the New York area to join at our festive table. The wonderful Norma cooked my favorite meal, turkey and stuffing, and took charge of all the loving preparations for fourteen people. I feel both humbled and grateful to be surrounded by an abundance of love and comfort.

Today is a joyous day for another reason. Today is my birthday and I turn thirty-one. This is a turning point because my mother was thirty-one when she received her terminal diagnosis, while I am blessed to be thirty-one and cancer-free. My mother and I may have shared similar fates for a time but clearly our destinies were never to be the same.

I thank God that despite all the suffering in this world I have been given another chance at life. Not everyone is so fortunate. This is a special day for me not only because it is Purim and my birthday, but also because I'm surrounded by family members who have prayed and wished for my recovery.

I pray, with all my heart and soul that God continues to watch and protect us. I count blessings every second. I see the hand of God throughout my day. Each and every day is filled with miracles, if I simply open my eyes. I hope and pray the pain we have experienced will finally subside and we will feel the true happiness that this day prescribes for us all.

EPILOGUE

Yeah, life after cancer is hard. My oncologist from Philadelphia was not returning my calls and so I changed to one in New York. The listlessness I felt was overwhelming. The thought of what I would do with myself felt catastrophic. I tried to focus energies on rebuilding my children's security from the time I was sick, but an evil thought overtook me: *What if this cancer comes back?*

It wasn't an unrealistic fear. My first PET scan three months after the last treatment had indicated activity in the area of my foot where the surgery had been done. In fact, as I was driving into the city that day, I was convulsively crying out of fear there might be *something* and this "unproven" treatment I had put my family and myself through would all be for nothing. In the car I tried to change my thoughts to a more positive approach and I prayed to God, "Thank you for giving me this opportunity to have this test so if there is *something* I can take care of it. But just one thing, God: I can handle any fight, you can challenge me again, but could you please give me time in between traumas?"

There had to be twelve hours before the PET scan of no caffeine, tobacco, or alcohol. The scan was scheduled for 9 AM the next day, so between 8 PM and 9 PM the night before I drank an entire bottle of wine and then passed out. I managed to calm myself enough to go through the PET scan, but on the way home I felt a mole on my head and started to panic. To me if felt larger than usual and I began to think I had a new Melanoma. It was Friday afternoon. I paged my dermatologist, who is also an Orthodox Jew, two hours before Shabbat. I waited by the phone eagerly. She had told me on many occasions that I could always call her and she would make herself available. I figured this was an emergency. She finally called me back within an hour before Shabbat and I told her about the mole on my head. Very calmly she told me she had been watching that mole in the past and it probably wasn't anything. I told her it felt bigger and that I had an appointment to see my surgical oncologist — the one who had made me upset back in the fall — on Monday. She said, "If it's anything, your doctor will look at it on Monday."

I was not comforted. I built up nerve and asked the question for which I feared a rejection: "Could I just please drive over to your house and you could take a quick look at it?" She answered curtly, "It's too close to Shabbat and I have to get my children ready. Anyway, if it's anything there's nothing that could be done until Monday."

I took in a big gulp of air and answered, "Thank you," and got off the phone. Josh was sitting next to me while I was on the phone, also eager to hear what she had to say. As soon as I got off the phone I started bawling.

Josh asked, "What did she say?"

I said, "SHE SAID NO!"

"What do you mean she said, no," he said.

"I mean, SHE SAID, NO THAT I COULDN'T GO OVER TO HER HOUSE!" I then went to my bathroom and took a valium.

Josh was upset and nervous and I was freaking out. I had never asked her for anything. There are so many doctors in my neighborhood that I have visited on Shabbat either for myself or for my children who have willingly sacrificed their time for me, just as they would do for anyone else. I questioned myself if I was wrong to expect this from her. After all, I only lived five minutes away. Yes, I knew that this was a psychological issue, but after all that I've been through, which she clearly knew, I had hoped for some mercy or kindness.

Even the doctor I was planning to see on Monday had given me his home and cell number to let me feel I could call him for anything. I was hurt, devastated, let down. I tried to make excuses for her that she needed to separate work and family but, when I called my sister Deborah and told her what happened, she was disgusted. I thought she could give an objective opinion as the wife of a doctor. I wondered how he would respond to this type of call.

Deborah answered, "Do you know how many times Marc has gotten up in the middle of the night to answer the silliest of questions? This should not have been a big deal."

Josh and I spent the Shabbat not talking about it further, holding in our thoughts and fears.

Monday was the first time I would see my surgical oncologist since the diagnosis. I had thought of switching doctors as I did with my regular oncologist, but wanted to give this relationship a chance because he had always treated me with the utmost respect. When I saw him, I said that I had second thoughts about coming back to him.

Immediately I saw the sad look on his face and he said, "Why?"

I told him he had let me down. He had told me there were no longer amputations for melanoma and he hadn't prepared me. Up until then he had been my hero. He saved me and cured me through the first melanoma.

I could tell he was sincere and he said, "If I knew this was how you felt I would have called. But because you went and did your treatment somewhere else I was no longer part of the team. Your situation was highly irregular as in the foot there was very little tissue left and the only thing to do in the end was remove the bones. I'm so sorry."

As I sat there crying I was so happy I had come back to him because he really is a caring man and doctor. I also was proud of myself that I confronted him and didn't simply run away.

With this experience behind me, when I got home I called the dermatologist's office and told the receptionist I would no longer be seeing this doctor and would like a copy of my records. She asked why and I told her, but I asked her not to tell the doctor my reasons, hoping she would call. The next day I picked up my records and the doctor never called.

The next day I had an appointment to meet a new dermatologist, someone highly recommended in my neighborhood, who also happens to be a member of the synagogue I attend. We met and he has treated me with compassion ever since. I feel assured that if I called him five minutes before Shabbat or even on Shabbat, he would never tell me he was unable to see me.

That Friday I went for a follow-up to my surgical oncologist who told me the results of my PET scan. He was concerned about the area of my foot that lit up on the scan. His first assumption was that surgery and trauma to the area could cause the scan to light up, but his responsibility as my doctor was to prove this was so.

I asked him, "What would it mean if this was another Melanoma?"

He said, "Unfortunately it would mean that your treatment was not successful and we would have to remove more of your foot."

I asked him to point to where it would need to be amputated. He explained that either it could be removed up until the ankle—as the "Chopper" doctor originally suggested, but he felt it would be much safer if my lower leg was removed up to the bottom of my knee. He said it would make a better fit for a prosthetic.

I sat there calmly. Anyhow, the doctor said that he didn't want to pursue it just yet and that I should have another PET scan in three months to observe for changes. I left his office a little shell-shocked and on my way home I practiced driving with my left leg. There was no way that this was going to stop me from being independent and driving my car.

Of course this was not news that Josh was looking forward to hearing either, but we had no choice but to do what we have become accustomed to, *waiting*. And in between the waiting we would have to push the fears to the back of our heads and live life to the fullest, try our best to be happy, and give the most that we could to our children. It wasn't a death sentence yet, but it did feel like something was looming over us. I think we had just hoped for a break, a small respite from cancer.

But as my doctor said, "Julie, this is going to be the rest of your whole long life. Because you have had this disease twice, anything that is suspicious behooves me to look into it. You'll just have to get used to it." Well, Josh and I were not used to it yet, but God, over time, gives us the gift of forgetfulness—now I just pray for that time.

APPENDIX
Thanks

We are blessed to live in the community of the Five Towns. I only hope that when I get better I, too, can volunteer and cook for others. It is such a wonderful gift to give to someone in need—it makes me feel I am not alone. I have also been inundated with phone calls that I can't possibly return but it's nice to know that people are thinking of me. My greatest comfort comes from learning that people are praying for me. Medical studies have shown that patients who were prayed for recovered faster than those who were not.

Since I have been sick, the community hasn't stopped bringing meals and flowers, and sending teenagers over to play with our children. People volunteer to drive me to doctors' appointments, pick my kids up from school, make play-dates with them, and even help get my kids to their after-school activities.

When my mother-in-law moved in she was so pleasantly surprised at the amount of *chesed* (kindness) the community has extended to our family that she wrote about it in her column in the *Canadian Jewish News*, January 8, 2004:

Chesed and Community   By Norma Joseph

It has become fashionable to be disheartened by the present state of our

Jewish community. Criticism abounds about deficiencies in community spirit and communal action, and many young Jews do not even want to work for community organizations.

Given that state of affairs, I want to tell you a good-news story. Don't get me wrong. There is plenty to find fault with and a great deal of improvement is needed. But there is also much that can convey respect and pride.

Recently, my family has been the recipient of an outpouring of a unique kind of Jewish kindness – chesed. Chesed is not easily translated. Many define the word as "acts of kindness," or of "loving kindness, mercy and benevolence."

But it means much more. One of God's attributes is chesed. Biblical Ruth was repeatedly complimented for her acts of chesed to both the dead and the living.

The term refers to deeds that are clearly above and beyond normal human decency or beneficence. Justice is necessary, but we humans could not survive without the linked notions of chesed and rachamim, mercy and compassion. That is one of Judaism's primary convictions. Traditionally, we describe care of the dead as an act of chesed shel emet, kindness of the truest sort. Anticipating no payback, we care for the deceased with the purest and most selfless of motivations.

So we have a history and a tradition of accepting, and even expecting, that periodically members of our community will step forward and display an inordinate sense of compassion and human kindness – kindhearted souls who redeem us all.

From New York to Boston to Montreal, I have seen individual Jews and communal organizations reach out to us without even knowing us. They heard that we were in a crisis and they wanted to help. Actually, in the religious community, people just said they wanted to do chesed. At one point we tried to stop the flow, but were told we could not: too many people had already lined up. This was their chesed and how could we be so selfish as to prevent that. Amazing!

I am not talking about a mass effort of considerable or comprehensive action, but rather about small deeds, little acts that slowly accumulate and make life easier or more comfortable. People willing to drive, to do carpool, to play with the kids, to say hello, to shop, to pray and to let us know that they care.

Most notably, since my daughter-in-law took ill, dinner has arrived every night. Quietly and consistently, this small gesture by numerous women has filled my world with chesed. It is such a small thing, yet it is so substantive and far-reaching. I am in awe and grateful

The hard thing about all this 'receiving' is that I often feel I don't have close friends. I live in a community where many have known each other since their youth and I feel shy about breaking in. In spite of my loneliness, my friend Jordana wrote me this letter:

Julie –

I always knew you were an incredibly special person with magnetism that attracts all who meet you. It is at these trying times that your special qualities shine through and others are given the opportunity to express their love, concern, and respect for you. Here is just a smattering of informal grassroots things that I randomly heard of that have occurred to aid you in your full and speedy recovery.

Tehillim (reciting Psalms for the sick) groups were specifically organized the day of your surgery in the Five Towns, Riverdale, North Shore High School Faculty, and the Stellla K. Abraham High School for Girls. Tehillim were said at the Kotel (the Western Wall) and in yeshivot (academies for Jewish learning) in Israel, including Midreshet Lindenbaum and Gush Etzion. Your name was also presented to rabbis worldwide. The book of Tehillim was completed multiple times by your friends this past week. Shmirat ha Loshen (groups formed to avoid gossiping) in Jerusalem and Raanana were formed in your honor. You are loved by all who encounter you and may Hashem hear all of our tefillot (prayers)!

– Jordana

I feel grateful for Jordana's letter and the efforts people have made on my behalf, but despite these efforts I still cry from feeling alone.

RESOURCES

Josh and I began listening to the audio tape of a book that our sister-in-law Yael, who is married to Josh's brother Ami, had given him called *The Power of Now* by Eckhart Tolle, which discusses the possibilities for joy inherent in each moment; to appreciate the gift of our life.

I feel the same way when I go to my *Consegrity* therapist. She, too, practices the art of being in the *now* and explains we can only exist in this moment, because the past and future are beyond our control. As Tolle writes, the past and the future are illusory; all we have is this moment.

I also read Lance Armstrong's cancer memoir, *It's not About the Bike: My Journey Back to Life*. I purchased the book soon after my second diagnosis, though it took me months to be able to read anything longer than two pages. I was dying to read *The DaVinci Code* — in fact three different people bought me the book — but every time I began to read, I just couldn't get past the first few pages. My thoughts were constantly racing. Then there was so much in my mind between painkillers from surgery, and then the Biochemo drugs. When I picked up Armstrong's book, I was carried away. At first I was hesitant to read it because after having finished treatment I thought it would depress me further to read a cancer memoir, but his story and fight for life was so invigorating that it pushed me to work on my own writing. He had a story to tell and so did I. But what really made an impression on me was his chapter on "Survivorship", when he talks about life after cancer.

People encouraged me to prepare for things to do while I would be in treatment. I bought books on tape that I fell asleep to. I even purchased a computer with DVD capability so I could watch movies in the hospital. I would go to Blockbuster before each treatment and rent ten movies for the week, none of which I was actually able to watch completely.

My cancer had brought me back in touch with an old friend, who too was going through Melanoma and treatment. When she passed away, may her memory be blessed, in response to her obituary I wrote this letter to Editor of the *Jewish Week*.

Ode To Joy

When I attended Midreshet Lindenbaum in Israel from 1991 to 1993, I knew Joy Rochwarger-Balsam and was in awe of her (Obituary, May 28). Not only was she learned, she studied privately with Nechama Leibowitz. And she always made time for tennis.

When I returned to the U.S., I lost touch with Joy until this past November. I was searching for a treatment to my stage IV malignant melanoma and was put in touch with Joy. She was so optimistic. I told her how sad I was when I found out about her and she said, "I don't want anyone feeling bad for me because that's negative energy and I need to surround myself with positive energy."

I took mussar (inspiration) from that statement even though our situations were different. She was newly married and I was a mother of three children, aged 5 and younger.

Joy died from malignant melanoma, a lethal skin cancer that has no cure and most of its treatments are still in clinical trials. As a melanoma survivor who still has a 60 percent risk of recurrence, I feel more people need to learn about this often preventable disease.

In memory of Joy, who gave so much to the Jewish community, please put sunscreen on your children. The sun may feel good, but it is dangerous and deadly. I beg every parent to take their child's skin seriously because you might be able to prevent that fastest growing cancer for people in their 20s.

Lastly, when I would feel down and depressed and ask myself what is the purpose of all this mess I would think about the following quote from Rabbi Joseph Soloveitchik, z"l, and it would help me refocus what I felt my role was in this world and how I can make this terrible experience into a positive one.

> *Man's task in the world, according to Judaism, is to transform fate into destiny; a passive existence into an active existence; an existence of compulsion, perplexity and muteness into an existence replete with a powerful will, with resourcefulness, daring and imagination... "I ask one simple question: what must the sufferer do so that he may live through his suffering?" ... We do not inquire about the hidden ways of the Almighty, but , rather, about the oath wherein the man shall walk when suffering strikes. We ask neither about the cause of evil nor about its purpose, but rather about how might it be mended and elevated. How shall a person act in a time of trouble? What ought a man to do so that he not perish in his afflictions?*
>
> *The Halakhic (Jewish legal) answer to this question is very simple. Afflictions come to elevate a person, to purify and sanctify his spirit, to cleanse and purge it of the dross superficiality and vulgarity, to refine his soul and to broaden his horizons. The Halakhah (Jewish law) teaches us that the sufferer commits a grave sin if he allows his troubles to go to waste and remain without meaning or purpose.*[1]

---

[1] J.B. Soloveitchik, *Kol Dodi Dofek: It Is the Voice of My Beloved That Knocketh*, trans, L. Kaplan in B. H. Rosenberg and F. Heuman (eds.) Theological and Halakhic Reflections of the Holocaust, Hoboken, N.J.: KTAV, 1992, pp. 54-56.